New Directions in Theology Today

VOLUME VI

Man: The New Humanism

New Directions in Theology Today

WILLIAM HORDERN, GENERAL EDITOR

NEW DIRECTIONS IN THEOLOGY TODAY

Volume VI
Man: The New Humanism

BY
ROGER LINCOLN SHINN

Philadelphia
The Westminster Press

LIBRARY OF CONGRESS CATALOG CARD NO. 68–12256

Published by The Westminster Press ®
Philadelphia, Pennsylvania

PRINTED IN THE UNITED STATES OF AMERICA

TO

MY FATHER (1884–1965)

AND

MY MOTHER

Editor's Foreword

Theology always has existed in some tension with the church. But there is considerable evidence that today the gulf is wider than ever before. To both pastors and laymen it often seems that contemporary theology is working in opposition to the concerns of the parish. They are disturbed to read in newspapers and popular journals about theologians who seem to have lightly cast aside the cornerstones of the faith and who argue that the parish is doomed. To the theologian the parish often appears to be a respectable club dedicated to erecting buildings, raising budgets, and avoiding controversial issues.

There is little active dialogue between the theologian and the church today. The fault for this lies with both parties, but the situation is becoming increasingly serious as the church moves into a new age. This series is dedicated to the task of bridging the present gulf.

One of the reasons for the gulf between theology and the church is that neither the busy pastor nor the concerned layman can keep up to date with an ever-expanding theological literature. Thus, the purpose of New Directions in Theology Today is to present concise summaries of the present scene in theology. The series is not for the lazy

pastor, nor for the layman who is beginning his theological
education. Rather, these volumes are especially prepared
for the busy pastor who is concerned with keeping abreast
of modern theology and for the layman who, having been
initiated into theology, is reading for further study, particularly to find out what contemporary Christian thinkers
are saying.

The series is not written with the assumption that only
professional theologians have something to say, but is
offered in the hope that it will stimulate pastors and laymen to enter into the theological dialogue, and with the
conviction that a vital theology for our time must be the
work of the church as a whole.

WILLIAM HORDERN

Contents

Acknowledgments

This book includes the Rall Lectures, given at Garrett Theological Seminary, under the title "The New Humanism," in March, 1967. To that happy occasion I owe much of the stimulus for this book.

Behind the book lie other events during which I tested these ideas and revised them under criticism. Participants in those occasions will find echoes, direct and indirect, here. I list some of these in roughly chronological order, with thanks to the many people who helped me understand "the new humanism" and struggle with its meaning:

A lecture, "The Encounter with Humanism," at the Assembly of the International Congregational Council, Rotterdam, July, 1962.

A paper, "Responses to the Human Situation in the World Today," prepared for discussion at the Jewish-Christian Consultation, sponsored by the Synagogue Council of America and the World Council of Churches, Chateau de Bossey, Switzerland, August, 1965.

The Matzner Lectures on "Perplexities and Challenges in Christian Ethics," Wartburg Theological Seminary, February, 1967.

A series of lectures, "Existentialism and the New Humanism," Illinois Wesleyan University, March, 1967.

A paper, "The Ethics of Genetic Engineering," read at the Colloquium on the Implications of the Chemical-Biological Revolution, at North Dakota State University (cosponsored by Moorhead State College and Concordia College), April, 1967.

A conference with students from a dozen Midwestern colleges at the Yokefellow Institute, Richmond, Indiana, February, 1967; and two Easter sermons at the National Convention of the Intercollegiate Association of Women Students at West Virginia University, March, 1967.

To these I should add the constant stimulating criticism and discussion of my students at Union Theological Seminary and Columbia University.

R. L. S.

CHAPTER I

The Dynamics of Christian Thought About Man

From a German biologist comes a story that tells something about the condition of man in our time. There was once a man who discovered his shadow. Watching its lithe motion, he assumed that it was alive. Because it followed him so faithfully, he decided that it must be his servant. But gradually he began to believe that he was imitating the shadow. He took increasing account of its comfort and welfare. He awkwardly maneuvered himself in order that it might sit in a chair or lie in bed. Eventually the man became, in effect, "the shadow of his shadow."[1]

The story warns us that man is constantly struggling to understand himself and the relation between this self and its many images. Our age is going at the job in a peculiarly troubled, sometimes frantic way. A dazzling and bewildering history makes the effort both necessary and difficult. Man sees the frontiers of human power advance swiftly. He feels the lure and assault of new opportunities, new temptations, new ideas. Forces outside and inside himself demand that he fit expected roles and images. He wonders about the relation of himself to these roles and images. Is he the creator of the roles he plays, or is he reduced to being the image of his image?

He asks other questions. Is man the director or the plaything of his history? In this swift-moving world is our own human nature undergoing some change? Are the bulldozers that reshape the landscape also cutting a channel through the person and his selfhood? Do new technologies, strange creations of contemporary art, and transformed political structures express a revolution within man?

We do not know the answer to all these questions, but we can already recognize that this twentieth century is one of the momentous epochs in the human adventure of self-understanding. Man is exercising powers beyond the dreams of the past—powers of economic production, of exploration of space, of destructive warfare. He is forging new tools of inquiry into his own life and nature, tools of psychology, biochemistry, and genetics. He spins out new hopes and fears as he sees simultaneously the possibility of the conquest of hunger and poverty or of the self-destruction of the human race in thermonuclear disaster.

Christians in a time like ours must question and rethink their traditional faith. There is nothing disloyal—although there are loyal and disloyal ways—in doing so. Christian thought is not a theoretical science, ambitious to build a fixed structure to apply to all times and places. It is alive and mobile. Some themes that concerned men passionately in the past seem strangely dead today. Other insights of faith, neglected by generations of the recent past, leap into new prominence today.

Of course, Christian faith has qualities of constancy and continuity; otherwise there would be no possibility of distinguishing *Christian* thought from whim or idolatry. But even in its constancy the accent that is appropriate to one time may be unneeded in another. And the insight that any generation *discovers* will be far more powerful than the idea it *inherits,* even though the discovery may be of an old but long forgotten truth.

Theology is a human activity. Like any human activity it is partly an expression of the particular human culture in which it develops. It is also a response to that same culture. As an expression of culture it tends to *follow* the experiences and moods of its time and to say what the culture is saying. As a response to culture it seeks to *change* the ethos and thinking of its time and to say what the culture neglects to say or prefers not to hear.

Therefore it is not surprising that the Christian self-awareness and the Christian doctrine of man have gone through significant changes in recent decades—decades packed with historical and intellectual activity of many kinds. In this book I aim both to describe these changes and to give my own judgments of them.

PART ONE

The New Humanism

Chapter II

From Oxford to Geneva

In the still unfinished drama of self-understanding in the twentieth century we can begin to discern two acts. Both are incredibly complex, with plots and subplots as rich and intricate as life itself. But each act reveals a dominant theme. Act I, marking the first half of the century, brought a blasting of confident expectations and an utterly convincing demonstration of man's capacity for depravity and cruelty. Act II, which thus far marks the second half of the century, shows signs of a recovery of morale, a renewed celebration of the dignity of man.

Christians have shared this history with their fellowmen. They are spared nothing, and they occupy no privileged position. Insofar as they live by faith, they recognize, as they confront Jesus Christ, both their own misery and their own grandeur. Rarely, if ever, do they see both with equal power. In the first half of the current century they discovered anew, reluctantly and bitterly, the misery of man—his arrogance, his cowardice, his untrustworthiness—and his need for the grace of divine forgiveness. Now they are discovering again, sometimes timidly and sometimes brashly, that God can do a healing and creating work in man.

We can see something of the difference between the two acts by comparing two symbolic events: the Oxford Conference on Church, Community and State (1937) and the Geneva Conference on Church and Society (1966). Both these assemblies of Christians sought to discern the meaning of faith for the world of public affairs, and both called on Christians to enter into the struggles of man for peace and justice. But the two conferences show a notable difference in *élan*. In pointing to the contrast, I do not argue that either conference is superior to the other. Rather, I maintain that we can learn from both—and from the difference.

At Oxford everyone was aware of the growing menace of Nazism. The conference, recognizing the absence of the Evangelical Church in Germany, took note of the "affliction" of that church in its struggle against "distortion and suppression of Christian witness." The Message of the conference to the churches began: "We meet at a time when mankind is oppressed with perplexity and fear. Men are burdened with evils almost insupportable and with problems apparently insoluble."

Oxford, therefore, issued a call to repentance. "We do not call the world to be like ourselves," said the Message, "for we are already too like the world." From Oxford many churchmen took a rallying cry, "Let the church be the church."

In its lifting up of the vocation of the church, Oxford did not isolate the church from the world. On the contrary, it asked the church to take up its work of reconciliation in the world. A major part of that task, as many Christians saw it, was to bear "witness to an eternal truth and right" that might "help to save society from corruption and decay."[1]

When Oxford thought about man, it thought about his sin. Not *only* his sin, but *always* his sin. It recognized the worth and dignity of man, but it could never forget the atrocities he could commit. Reinhold Niebuhr in his influential address, "The Church Faces a Secular Culture,"[2] attacked the idolatries of secularism (idolatries of reason, race, and nation) and the sin of a church that failed to appreciate the passion for justice that sometimes appeared in secular forms. In one of the study volumes for the conference, a symposium on *The Christian Understanding of Man,* the "neo-orthodox" contributors hammered hard the theme of sin and guilt, while the more "liberal" writers corrected the excessive optimism in their theological tradition.

The history that followed Oxford vindicated the worst fears of men. Human nature demonstrated its depravity so convincingly that nobody alert to his world could miss the point. The contemporary generation has seen wars, hot and cold, massacres, racial persecution and violence, large-scale starvation, deliberate and refined cruelty, the feverish struggle for ever more devastating weapons, and the massive use of technology by governments more intent to put a man on the moon than to find homes and food for millions of poor people.

Conceivably, Christians might have responded by withdrawing from the world and looking for a haven in the church. Some took that response, and others remained as indifferent as they could to the momentous social changes of their time. But churchmen also saw other possibilities. They saw promise as well as threat in the movement of the world. Less and less did they ask the question: How can Christians witness to the eternal truth that may save society from corruption? More and more they asked: How does God's activity in the world offer his saving power to both world and church?

The World Council of Churches, planning the Geneva conference, chose the theme: "Christians in the Technical and Social Revolutions of Our Time." The delegates saw the dangers in the world, but they chose to accent the opportunities. So in their Message they said: "We have been reminded of the new possibilities now open before man, as well as of the new threats to human existence."

Talk of the dignity of man, which a generation earlier had been almost nostalgic and defensive, now was eager and militant. References to the future usually carried with them more hope than fear. Most of the spokesmen knew about the sinfulness of man; many testified to oppression, injustice, and bloodshed. But to any great emphasis upon sin, the reply was likely to be: "We understand that, but let's get on. What *else* can we say about man?"

Two words—*humanism* and *humanization*—resounded repeatedly at Geneva. Behind them was the conviction that, despite all the guilt we know so well, our humanity is something not to lament but to acclaim.

Humanism is a word that represents a long heritage in Western thought. In the Renaissance of the sixteenth century it stood for the rediscovery of the human and cultural values of the ancient world. In later centuries it came to take on a more militant meaning—an attitude that championed man *instead of* God. In 1933 a group of Americans issued "A Humanist Manifesto,"[3] calling on men to rely upon themselves rather than upon God, to seek human rather than divine values, to show confidence in scientific intelligence and its power to improve society.

The Manifesto appeared at a time when man was most obviously using his intelligence and scientific method to tyrannize other men. The words of the Manifesto soon sounded more forlorn than brave. The distinguished Columbia University professor, Frederick J. E. Woodbridge, wrote in 1940: " 'Humanism' today often suggests a polite superiority of character or a pleasant medicine for that spiritual nostalgia which sickens the soul when faith has apparently lost its foundations."[4] Theologians attacked humanism for the lack of the very quality it had boasted of possessing—realism.

From Geneva in 1966, however, the church heard a worldwide paean to humanism. John C. Bennett, summarizing a volume of preparatory documents for the conference, pointed to "a strong Christian humanism" expressed by many writers.[5] From Germany, H. D. Wendland asked that society be ordered "for the sake of man and for his human dignity"; and he asked for global responsibility as the expression of "a 'world-wide' humanism."[6] From India, Russell Chandran pointed to the possibility of cooperating with men of other religions in a "secular community based on common humanity."[7] From Japan, Yoshiaki Iisaka wrote: "The human is the measure of all things, because God became human in Jesus Christ."[8] From Czechoslovakia, J. M. Lochman recalled the "divine humanism" of the Bible (Matt. 25:40).[9] Later from the platform at Geneva, Dr. Lochman advocated "unconditioned humanism"—a humanism that comes from "Christ's commandment for unconditional solidarity with all men."[10]

Recognizing the many threats of our world to humanity, Geneva repeatedly called for the humanization of life and the institutions in which life is involved. Helmut Gollwitzer expressed a common conviction in his declaration: "The right social contribution of Christians is always and everywhere directed toward the humanizing of society."[11] The most dangerous effects of modern war, technology, and mass society were often described as dehumanization. The writings and addresses of Geneva sometimes referred to Paul Lehmann's theological ethic, built upon the effort to discover "what God is doing in the world to make and to keep human life human."[12]

Oxford 1937 and Geneva 1966 are convenient reference points for checking the movement of Christian thought about man in one generation. I do not want to exaggerate the difference. The Messages of both gatherings called for repentance and for responsible Christian activity in the world. The two Messages ended with the identical word from Scripture: "I have overcome the world." But something had happened between Oxford and Geneva. It could be called the rise of a new humanism.

To evaluate this new humanism is a major task. Even to define it is difficult. This book, rather than starting with a definition, works toward one. But since I use the term often in this book, I can immediately propose a tentative definition. Humanism is the appreciation of man and of the values, real and potential, in human life. It esteems man—not as an animal, a machine, or an angel, but as man. It is concerned with the agonies and triumphs of the human spirit, not in any racial or religious or intellectual elite, but in the whole range of history and experience. It may be humble or haughty, accurate or mistaken in its judgments, but always it cherishes humanity.

Such a definition may seem so inclusive that nobody would want to be left out. But a look at contemporary history shows many attacks upon humanism. In racial, political, and religious pride we see "man's inhumanity to man."[13] In fascinated devotion to the machine, man may enslave himself to the product of his own skills. In the lust for wealth he may burn out himself and his fellow-men. Humanism, far from being a consensus, is always embattled.

Humanism, in this tentative definition of it, may be characteristic of Christians, Jews, Muslims, Hindus, Buddhists, agnostics, avowed atheists. Yet men with all these labels may be humanists or antihumanists. In fact, one of the issues for any of the historic religions is how it understands its own distinctiveness and its own community of faith in relation to mankind.

In this chapter I have pointed to the emergence of a humanism, long subdued but recently outspoken, within the Christian community. To understand and assess the change, in its subtlety and its boldness, we must trace the story in more detail.

CHAPTER III

Reasons for the New Humanism

We can never say precisely why the words and ideas that dazzle one generation are pale to another. Historical causation, above all in the history of human thought and spirit, is not a precise science—partly because causation is immensely complex and partly because human freedom acts upon all causes.

But we can readily point to some aspects of the history of our times that provide reasons for the changing insights into man. For convenience we can identify five such contributions to the new humanism.

1. *Achievements and opportunities.* "Now, for the first time in human history, all people are convinced that the benefits of culture ought to be and actually can be extended to everyone."[1] In those words the Second Vatican Council expressed a powerful conviction of the new humanism. After centuries of painful history, man has found the possibility of defeating his ancient enemies—hunger, poverty, and drudgery. That he has not yet done so is desperately clear. But he knows how.

Science and technology have brought the possibilities. Despite man's fumbling and inept uses of them, his new powers are stupendous.

Man once commanded the power of his muscles, then of his domesticated animals. Today he touches a switch to bring electrical power into his home, and his industry taps the immense powers of nuclear energy. Once he could travel only the distances he could walk; now in a day he can soar into space, circle the earth a few times, and return. Once he gathered information from his senses plus the little that other people might tell him. Now he sits in his living room, watching and listening to events in far parts of the world.

The swift advances of recent years give men the excitement of living in a new age. Everyone has the experience of doing things never done by any past generation. People live with the expectation of continuous new accomplishments. Many of yesterday's impossibilities are commonplace happenings today. What men once begged the gods to do, they now do for themselves.

We do not yet know whether man is wise or compassionate enough to use his powers for his own benefit. But we do know that the possibilities are immense. Opportunities once available to none, or only to the privileged few, are open to many. Man would be dull indeed if he did not marvel at his attainments. Human vision turned into deed is one reason for the new humanism.

2. *Historical crises.* New powers have brought new fears. Some historical events of recent experience have so threatened humanity as to remind this race of mankind that its human heritage is both precious and precarious. The events that endanger life and culture call men to vindicate the cause they all share.

Paul Goodman, one of our more stimulating social critics, has made this catalog of devastating events:

With dismaying rapidity during the past 30 years, society has become dehumanized. One can tick off the horrors: the Spanish War, World War II, the gas chambers, the atom bomb, the cold war, the stockpiling of atom bombs, the Frankenstein-monster technology, the unecological urbanization, the cumbersome centralization, the social engineering, the mass communications, the processing education, the trivializing of democracy.[2]

Not everybody will agree with this entire polemic. Some, as I shall point out later, are more enthusiastic advocates of contemporary culture. But everybody can pick a few impressive items from Goodman's list. Such an indictment prompts a double response. It shows us the desperation of our historical predicament and it alerts us to the uniquely human attainments and possibilities that are under attack.

Certainly the Nazi movement was a crime against humanity. The slaughter of six million Jews was an offense not only against the Jewish people but against mankind. The disregard for persons, the calculated cruelty, the distortion of human life were an assault upon humanity. Such an attack reminded people that life and culture are real and valuable. It rallied men of many faiths and purposes, men who shared little except their common human nature, to struggle for the sake of man.

More recently the civil rights movement in the United States has demonstrated that the degradation of men because of race or color is an offense against humanity. In the conflict we have seen human dignity abused. We have also seen human dignity assert itself against abuse. Some of us, seeing men of another color demonstrate their courage, have found a new satisfaction in the humanity we shared with them.

Thus the very events that have exposed the viciousness of men, that have shaken any confidence that men are good-natured and generous, have shown us the value of humanity and the possibility that men of diverse races and creeds can unite around a concern which is human. William Faulkner, responding to the Nobel award in literature for 1949, expressed the faith that man would both *endure* and *prevail*. Faulkner was not voicing the glib confidence in progress of an earlier humanism or the cheerful expectation that modern industry would raise the standard of living for everybody. He was looking into the face of the fateful and tragic aspects of life, yet celebrating the magnificence that he saw in the often foolish and brutal society of men. He was speaking for a new style of humanism.

3. *The dehumanizing effects of institutions.* Paul Goodman's list of portentous movements in recent history includes not only the vicious blows and intrigues against men. He sees also the threat in many of the movements commonly associated with social and economic progress: the advance of technology, urbanization, social engineering, and mass communications.

Such processes are transforming the conditions of life all over our globe. They shatter and restructure tribal societies that have followed traditional folkways for generations. They change the patterns of life and power structures of great cities. They upset established relations between young and old, employer and employee, man and woman. Nobody yet understands fully their present impact, much less their potentialities.

Modern technology is in some ways a liberating force. The institutions that accompany it sometimes protect persons and enlarge opportunities. But many people, like Paul Goodman, ask whether all these forces are dehumanizing us. Are they routinizing, mechanizing, homogenizing, sorting out, and classifying persons? Does mass production extend itself to the production of personality? Does mass communication impose itself upon us rather than serve our personal interests?

We cannot always be sure. Change means loss as well as gain. Are the losses simply of the familiar or are they of the valuable? We hardly know how to answer such a question in a time when the criteria of values are themselves shifting.

Perhaps in the long run promise will outweigh threat. But we know the threat is real. We resist the invasion and subjection of our personhood. Sometimes we capitulate. Sometimes we assert our humanity.

4. *The awareness of religious pluralism.* Increasingly, people rub elbows with other people of different religious traditions and beliefs. They find that persons of diverse religious faiths share—that is, they must share and sometimes want to share—some common problems and some common purposes.

As recently as 1940, Winston Churchill could declare that upon the Battle of Britain depended "the survival of Christian civilization."[3] The lingering notion of Christendom persisted in the church and colored much social thinking. Today, Churchill's words have a nostalgic sound —no less to the church than to society at large.

In some parts of the world the idea of Christendom never made sense. The development of the ecumenical movement has given an increasingly conspicuous voice to Christians who come from parts of the world where there never was a Christendom and there is no expectation that there will be one.

How, for example, shall the Christians of India contribute to the needs of that society? Not by becoming a Christian pressure group, whose influence is negligible.

However meaningful the life of the Christian community for its members, its public impact depends upon working with men of goodwill, whatever their religious convictions. So M. M. Thomas of India, chairman of the Geneva Conference on Church and Society, said that contemporary developments demand "a Christian social ethic which assimilates and is more challengingly relevant to the new secular humanism."[4]

In Western Europe and America, the lands that once formed a sort of Christendom, religious diversity is increasingly obvious. In 1931 a United States Supreme Court could say that we are "a Christian people."[5] That is not the language of the court or of public discourse today. Christians, impelled by their faith, join forces with many of differing faiths to make this a better society not for the church or for Christians but for people.

There are, of course, many traps and illusions in the tendency to depreciate specific faith and to elevate some morality that seeks a common ground. Christian faith— and, I suppose, most historic faiths—has a bite and a delight unknown to those who settle for the common faith of all right-minded conformists. But there is, within Christian faith itself, an impulse toward the new humanism; and that will be our next point.

5. *Biblical theology.* While all the foregoing movements were going on, Christians were continuing to study their Scriptures. The theologies of the generation just past had rediscovered the uniqueness of the Biblical revelation, had led Christians to disentangle the Biblical message from the many voices of culture, had insisted that God is as truly the judge as the sustainer of human enterprises. Sometimes these insights led Christians to glory in their distinctiveness from culture.

But Biblical studies led to further discoveries. Some

Biblical assertions, muted in the recent past and perhaps through centuries of history, have leaped into the consciousness of contemporary Christians.

Thus Christians became aware, as often they have not been aware, that the mission of the church, although clearly a unique mission, is directed toward the world. They found that Jesus Christ came, not to make people Christians—he did not use or know the word—but to declare God's love and forgiveness to sinners. They found Paul's declaration, "In Christ God was reconciling the world to himself" (II Cor. 5:19). They found that the Bible declares an incarnation of the divine word in human flesh and a victory of God over evil, acts which have significance for all men. "And all flesh shall see the salvation of God." (Luke 3:6.)

Such insights need not wash out into some nondescript syncretism. The very intense awareness of the Christian mission leads believers to increased concern for "all flesh." It leads, that is, to a new humanism.

These five historical forces, and perhaps many others, give impetus to the new humanism. Not all of them operate with equal force among all advocates of the new humanism, but all of them are at work.

CHAPTER IV

Some Leaders in the Change

Paul Tillich, examining theology in the nineteenth and twentieth centuries, observed that all modern theology is an attempt to unite two trends in Christian thinking— the classical (or orthodox) and the humanistic. Summarizing the history of Christian thought in these centuries, he said:

So the whole story has a dramatic character. It is the drama of the rise of a humanism in the midst of Christianity which is critical of the Christian tradition, departs from it and produces a vast world of secular existence and thought. Then there is the rise of some of the greatest philosophers and theologians who try to unite these divergent elements again. Their syntheses in turn are destroyed and the divergent elements collide and try to conquer each other, and new attempts to reunite them have to be made.[1]

The great liberal theologies of the nineteenth and early twentieth centuries wrought a synthesis. It is important that they did so. The alternative was a retreat of Christianity into the ghetto, an isolation from the discoveries of modern science and the adventure of modern man. Liberal theology, especially in the social gospel, was concerned for man. It related Christian faith to the wholeness of life and the variety of human energies. It was a heroic effort, in some respects an irrevocable achievement.

In retrospect, however, we are likely to say that the victory came too easily. Sometimes, at least, the synthesis between Biblical faith and humanism meant the neglect of the genuine tension that Christianity has always seen between Christ and the world. Twentieth-century history disrupted all comfortable syntheses. When the modern world—whether bourgeois, Communist, or Nazi—said to Christianity, "Come, join us," some Christians found themselves compelled to answer, "No."

Theology, therefore, undertook a disrupting mission in this century. The labels of such theology—neo-orthodoxy, theology of crisis, dialectical theology—are not very helpful. More important is the fact that Christians were making a prophetic protest against destructive and idolatrous forces in the modern world. Not synthesis, but heroic opposition became the Christian task.

But opposition is never the living heartbeat of Christian faith. Even in those years when disentanglement and separation were a Christian vocation, the most thoughtful of Christians knew that their purpose was reimmersion in the life of men.

It would be false to say that the days of prophetic protest are past. Christian faithfulness, as truly as ever in history, requires opposition to the tyrannies and cajoleries of man. But in the aftermath of the momentous protests of the recent past and their distinction between the demands of God and the ways of men, Christians are seeking once again to understand and realize their identity with man. They are working out a new humanism.

This new humanism is emerging in immense variety. To see both its unity and its diversity, we must investigate it in several of its expressions. One of the leaders of the movement, whom I have already mentioned and to whom

I shall return, was Paul Tillich. But in this chapter I shall examine the humanistic motif in several other thinkers. Perhaps the most remarkable fact of this inquiry is that the earliest and the most notable of the new humanists are the very thinkers who led the rebellion against the earlier confident syntheses of liberal theology.

KARL BARTH'S CHANGE OF DIRECTION

Karl Barth is the Christian thinker who has given this century its most radical statement on the corruption of man and its most dramatic statement of Christian humanism. That the same man could do both is a story worth investigating.

Barth first impressed the world as the Swiss pastor and theologian who jolted modern man, already shaken by the experiences of World War I, with the news of the desperate situation of sinful men and their utter dependence upon God. In his ministry he discovered the banality of the clichés by which men and the church reassured themselves in the midst of a disastrous history. To the platitudes of conventional theology and popular wisdom he opposed, "with a joyful sense of discovery," the "mighty voice of Paul."[2] Barth's doctrine proclaimed the distance between God and man: "If I have a system, it is limited to a recognition of what Kierkegaard called the 'infinite qualitative distinction' between time and eternity, and to my regarding this as possessing negative as well as positive significance: 'God is in heaven, and thou art on earth.'"[3]

A powerful polemicist, Barth asserted the depravity of man and the grace of God, who in Jesus Christ saved man quite apart from any lingering goodness or potentiality of man. In his famous reply to Emil Brunner in 1934, he granted that man was not a tortoise or a cat, but insisted that he was "a sinner through and through," that he could claim no "capacity for revelation," no "point of contact" for encounter with God. If God encounters and forgives man, the reason is not in some human potentiality but in God's act which creates the possibility of a relationship.[4]

Barth's ideas provoked strenuous opposition, but he became increasingly influential as the Nazi tyranny, World War II, and the aftermath of war proved beyond much possibility of doubt that man was capable of terrifying evil. Plainly, civilization had not vanquished savagery. The heritage of humane and Christian ideals had little evident effect upon the behavior of nations and peoples. In the face of the overwhelming facts there was not much point in bucking up human confidence by muttering that man is basically good but has some lingering bad impulses and habits, or that education will overcome the ignorance that still holds back the human race. Most people learned to recognize the depravity of man, at least in their enemies; Barth helped many to recognize it also in themselves.

But by the time Barth's message about man got through most effectively, his thought was already taking a new turn. His withering description of man apart from God was giving way to a Christian humanism. Although he argued his case against Nazism on a clearly theological and Christological basis, he was capable of appealing to a simple human courage. "The world needs men," he said in his Gifford Lectures, "and it would be sad if it were just the Christians who did not wish to be men."[5] Of his decision to oppose the Nazis, he wrote: "It is a choice where I would rather say 'No' with the crudest democratically-minded fellow citizen than 'Yes' or 'Yes and No' with the most pious fellow-Christian!"[6] In such sayings Barth showed an earthiness and humanity that had not always come through in his writings.

During and after the war Barth's latent humanism moved out into the open. In 1949 he described his own history by saying: "To say 'yes' came to seem more important than to say 'no' (though that is important, too)."[7] That same year he gave an address entitled "The Christian Message and the New Humanism."[8] In it he declared: "The Christian message is the message of the humanism of God." To his largely secular audience he stated his conviction that his esteem for man was not due to anything "inherent in the nature of man" but to the specific Christian faith that "God and man are one in Jesus Christ." Thus on God's free grace Barth based his humanism.

In the following years Barth developed this conception at length in his massive *Church Dogmatics*. But never did he state it more clearly than in a brief essay of 1956 entitled "The Humanity of God."[9] With candor and good humor he acknowledged a major change in the direction of his theology. He recalled that in his early career he had emphasized the *deity* and the distance of God, that he had assaulted theological error with "a derisive laugh" instead of "a sad and friendly smile," that he had chastized man and "boxed his ears" with the concept of a God who is "wholly other." While maintaining that his effort had been right and necessary in its time, Barth saw it in retrospect as "more like the report of an enormous execution than the message of the Resurrection, which was its real aim."[10]

Now, wrote Barth, against that recognition of the deity of God, it is possible to assert his humanity. In his characteristic style Barth piled up the phrases to make his point:

It is precisely God's *deity* which, rightly understood, includes his *humanity.* . . . In Jesus Christ there is no isolation of man from God or of God from man. . . . How could God's deity exclude His humanity, since it is God's freedom for love and thus His capacity to be not only in the heights but also in the depths, not only great but also small, not only in and for Himself but also with another distinct from Him, and to offer Himself to him? . . . His deity *encloses Humanity in itself.* . . . It would be the false deity of a false God if in His deity His humanity did not also immediately encounter us. . . . In Him [Jesus Christ] the fact is once for all established that God does not exist without man. . . . God is *human.*[11]

If we challenge Barth's consistency over the years, he is not in the least disturbed. He once described his career as a "succession of present moments."[12] Yet he could, if he wanted, point to one consistent quality in his theology. From beginning to end everything has hinged on the Biblical revelation, centering in Jesus Christ. In this sense his humanism has nothing in common with the high estimates of man's abilities, so frequently heard in popular culture. It is not based on observations of man in general. It rests strictly and solely on Jesus Christ.

But this does not mean that it is for Christians alone or that Christians have any privileged status. God's affirmation of man in Christ is an affirmation of humanity—not of good men or religious men or Christian men. Barth has no interest in the various religions and irreligions of the world, but he is interested in *men* of all religions and no religions. Christians are not more human and not more loved of God than anyone else, but Christians have a peculiar vocation. For it is the Christian church that recognizes, delights in, celebrates, and witnesses to the humanity of God.[13]

The Impact of Dietrich Bonhoeffer

Before Karl Barth discovered the humanity of God—or at least before he declared it clearly to the world—Dietrich Bonhoeffer was coming to still more radical conclusions. A prisoner of the Nazis, he sketched out his ideas in a few cryptic and tantalizing letters, written in the final months before his execution in 1945. For a time his thoughts remained hidden from all except a few friends. After they were published—in German in 1951 and in English in 1953—they exerted a dramatic seminal power. Many a person today has heard more quotations from a score of pages in Bonhoeffer than from shelves of writings by more recent Christian authors.

In prison Bonhoeffer met men of various nationalities and faiths. He studied the Bible, prayed, sometimes led worship and preached. Out of his experience came an intense concern for men—not a concern for Christians but a Christian concern for men, and a reassessment of what it means to be a Christian.

Bonhoeffer's humanism is expressed in two phrases that have become famous: "to be a man" and "the man for others." Let us here look at each in turn. (In the next chapter I shall point to other of his phrases and ideas.)

"To be a man" is the Christian vocation. But rather than wrench the phrase out of context, let us look at Bonhoeffer's own use of it:

To be a Christian does not mean to be religious in a particular way, to cultivate some particular form of asceticism (as a sinner, a penitent or a saint), but to be a man. It is not some religious act which makes a Christian what he is, but a participation in the suffering of God in the life of the world. (July 18, 1944.)

Jesus does not call men to a new religion, but to life. (July 18, 1944.)

The Christian is not a *homo religiosus,* but a man, pure and simple, just as Jesus was man, compared with John the Baptist anyhow. (July 21, 1944.)[14]

To people bored with religious piety and stodgy churchmanship, the phrase "to be a man" rang with a liberating power. Too often the modern generation had confused the Christian life with effete behavior and an inhibited humanity. Bonhoeffer's words stirred many a response. They became the title of one book, the inspiration for others.[15] They helped many people, especially young people, to get out of their ruts and see the Christian life as a bold adventure.

Inevitably some simplified and distorted the idea. In the first of the paragraphs I have quoted above, they stopped at the end of the first sentence—suppressing the next words about "participating in the suffering of God in the life of the world." But Bonhoeffer's own cruel death made it impossible to keep his words about suffering suppressed. His constant references to Jesus were a warning that "to be a man" was not simply to live a free and easy life.

In Bonhoeffer (as in Barth) everything centers in Jesus. So we come to the second of his phrases, "the man for others." Here was a humanistic description of Jesus. He was "one whose only concern is for others." Through him we realize that our own relation to God is "a new life for others, through participation in the Being of God."[16]

This humanistic Jesus is equally a divine Jesus. Jesus is "God in human form, . . . man existing for others, and hence the Crucified."[17]

Dietrich Bonhoeffer warned against some of the misinterpretations that came later. He disliked "the cult of the human," either as human pride or as the self-conscious cultivation of personal relations. But he appreciated "the simple fact that people are more important in life than anything else." And he warned that for many people in the contemporary world "man is just a part of the world of things; the experience of the human simply eludes them." (August 10, 1944.)[18]

Thus it is fair enough to describe Bonhoeffer as a humanist, if we distinguish his beliefs from the tame and the self-indulgent forms of humanism that are familiar in our culture. His is a humanism in the tradition of the prophets and the martyrs.

THE HUMANISM OF REINHOLD NIEBUHR

In the United States, Reinhold Niebuhr has been, in some contexts, the penetrating critic of liberal humanism and, in other contexts, the champion of humanistic endeavors. His career shows no such climactic change of direction as Karl Barth's, but has characteristically moved in response both to public events and to intellectual inquiries. Niebuhr, living in the intersection of the political and scholarly worlds, has been the theological critic of humanism and the humanistic critic of theology.

In his intellectual pilgrimage, in which he became the chief mover of a theological revolution in America, Niebuhr drew into an intricate unity a variety of insights from diverse sources. With the social gospel he shared a concern for justice in industrial America. With Karl Marx he saw the functioning of power in social structures and analyzed the ways in which men's thoughts and actions, even when seemingly idealistic, are influenced by their place in the social scheme. With Augustine he came to see

mankind as a unity, in which all men are moved by their
loves and infected by sin, and to see history as the dramatic conflict between good and evil impulses that are
never entirely sorted out in terrestrial experience. With
Kierkegaard he probed the freedom, anxiety, and sin of
the individual person, who in his uniqueness differs from
all others.

All these streams of thinking came together in Niebuhr's
most comprehensive work, *The Nature and Destiny of
Man*.[19] This book, the Gifford Lectures of 1939, was both
a theological and a humanistic inquiry. It was theological
in its development of themes from the Biblical and Christian heritage and its use of the traditional symbols of the
image of God, the Fall, and original sin. But, it should be
noted, these were always vindicated by reference to experience, not to authority. The book was humanistic in
its exploration of culture and its appropriation of materials from a wide range of the arts and scholarly disciplines.

The contrast between Niebuhr and the work of Barth
and Bonhoeffer is most obvious on the issues of Christology. For Barth and Bonhoeffer, everything centers specifically in Christ. For Niebuhr the faith in God's revelation
and reconciling work in Christ is utterly important. Yet
Niebuhr is quite uninterested in the classical formulations of the doctrine of Christ, considering them more a
barrier than a clarification for faith.[20] His long personal
history of intimate cooperation with Jews and secularists
in political and social causes has led him to respect the
goodwill that he found among those who did not share
his Christian faith. A humanistic realism led Niebuhr to
refer to a "hidden Christ," who works among those who
are not Christians and may not be influenced by Christianity.[21]

Another humanistic theme in Niebuhr is his immense emphasis upon human freedom and the possibilities of human life. The Gifford Lectures have always offended the orthodox by their call for a synthesis of Renaissance and Reformation insights. From the Renaissance, Niebuhr draws the appreciation of human aspiration and the continuous "new possibilities of the good"; from the Reformation, the awareness of the power of sin to infect even man's best endeavors.[22] After *The Nature and Destiny of Man*, Niebuhr has developed further his humanistic motifs in a variety of books dealing with politics, international relations, history, social philosophy, and the nature of man. We can see the change of emphasis most easily by looking at two writings in which Niebuhr specifically revises some of his earlier judgments: the Preface to the paperback edition (1963) of *The Nature and Destiny of Man* and the short volume *Man's Nature and His Communities*.

Here Niebuhr suggests that he might better have avoided the language of "the Fall" and "original sin," because such terms fail to communicate with the contemporary secular mind; but he reasserts their meaning, vindicating it by analysis of contemporary history and experience.[23] More significant is his affirmation, not new but more clearly emphasized than in the past, of certain secular disciplines and values. Thus he says of his own essays: "They also embody increasingly the insights of the secular disciplines and reflect the author's increasing enthusiasm for the virtues of an open society which allows freedom to all religious traditions, and also the freedom to analyze and criticize all these traditions through the disciplines of an empirical and historical culture."[24]

Among the helpful secular disciplines he mentions particularly the psychology of Erik Erikson. Here he finds confirmation for many of his own insights but also the language for reformulating some of them.[25] Specifically he uses Erikson's concept of "basic trust" to clarify his own doctrine of faith. In so doing, he criticizes the theological tradition for exaggerating the distinction between "saving grace," transmitted through the community of faith, and "common grace," operating through ordinary human relationships.[26] In effect the "hidden Christ" of his earlier works has moved from the position of footnote or parenthetical comment to become a major theme of his later writings. Similarly he now accords to disciplined ambition and self-affirmation in man an appreciation uncharacteristic of his earlier works.[27]

By this movement of thought Niebuhr, who was once the scourge of overconfident humanism, has become a leader of the new humanism. I do not mean to say that he characteristically describes himself as a humanist—any more than Bonhoeffer did. I rather suggest that the term fits him better than the term "neo-orthodox"—to use another word that he has never used of himself, though some have used it of him. But unlike Barth and Bonhoeffer, who shifted direction markedly, Niebuhr represents a man whose humanistic impulses, always obvious in his social activism and always implicit in his doctrine, have come increasingly to the fore in his writings.

ROMAN CATHOLIC HUMANISM

One stimulus to the new humanism is the lively interchange of ideas among Protestants, Roman Catholics, and secularists. The next chapter will say something about secularization. Here I shall comment on the contribution of Catholicism.

In one sense Catholicism has for centuries aimed to be

humanistic. It has organized its thinking under the categories of nature and grace, defining both a natural and a supernatural (or a temporal and eternal) destiny for men. Mankind, it has taught, has the capacity to organize life, more or less effectively, for temporal ends, apart from Christian revelation. In "natural law" (the awareness of good and evil that comes from experience or reason apart from any specific revelation) and the ancient virtues defined by the Greeks and taken over into Christianity, man recognizes human good. A person or society who lives on this level is incomplete, because the eternal aim is missing; but such life is within its own limitations good. To the Roman Catholic the Protestant Reformation has often seemed to be antihumanistic because the Reformers, with their great emphasis on human sin, had less confidence in man's ability to know and do the good.

To the non-Catholic—and I cannot pretend to be anything else—this humanism has always been suspect, partly because of the ascetic tradition within Catholicism and partly because of the use of papal authority and power to stifle the human spirit. Especially in the past century, when human powers were bursting old bonds on every hand, the Vatican often tried to tighten up the chains. Pius IX in the famous *Syllabus Errorum* (1864) rejected religious liberty and "progress, liberalism, and civilization as lately introduced." There was, to be sure, a humanistic spirit in a few of the papal encyclicals, notably Leo XIII's *Rerum Novarum* (1891) and Pius XI's *Quadragesimo Anno* (1931). But between the two, Pius X, moved partly by the follies of Protestant and secular liberalism, imposed rigorous constraints and excommunications upon Catholic scholars.

But the humanistic roots of Catholic theology kept sending up new shoots. At a time when the word "humanism," especially in its American use, was primarily a polemical word, hostile to the historic faiths, Jacques Maritain published his book *True Humanism*.[28] He criticized severely bourgeois humanism as barren and Marxist atheism as really a false religion. But he went on to call for a "new humanism"—many years before I, forgetting about Maritain, chose that phrase as the title for this book. This new humanism, said Maritain, is an "integral humanism," "the humanism of the Incarnation."

To Maritain, Karl Barth's theology of those days was antihumanistic as it demanded "the annihilation of man before God."[29] Maritain called for "an evangelical attention to human things."[30] In a sense he asked for recognition of the autonomy of secular life. Here Christians should seek "a relative but very real earthly happiness" for men, "a state of justice, of amity and prosperity making possible for each the fulfilment of his destiny."[31] Yet Christian faith should "interpenetrate the world" and "vivify the things of time."[32]

Maritain is a good symbol of the speed of theological change within Catholicism. Writing during a conservative papacy, he was a liberalizing influence within the church. But in the era following the Second Vatican Council, Maritain is a conservative. To many a contemporary Catholic theologian, Maritain's vision of a new Christendom (albeit a society committed to religious liberty) is far too nostalgic. And Maritain has attacked with some bitterness the radical tendencies within current Catholicism.[33]

But Maritain's book was only one stage in what Canon Charles Moeller of the Curia has called "a series of humanist and Christian events stretching from 1925 to 1963."[34] A more dramatic part of the story was the "thundering entry into Christian thought and controversy"[35] of Teilhard de Chardin, the Jesuit paleontologist and theologian, whose ideas have so stimulated Catholicism, even though the Vatican forbade their publication during his own lifetime. (Teilhard died on Easter Sunday, 1955, and his many books have stirred energetic discussions since then.)

Teilhard looked for "the simultaneous rebirth of humanism and of Christianity."[36] In his own career he worked toward "a finally explicit form" of a neo-humanism on which, he believed, "our future salvation depends."[37] To express the cosmic meaning of his humanism, he coined the word "hominisation" to refer to (1) the initial "leap from instinct to thought" in the evolution of man on earth and (2) "the progressive phyletic spiritualisation in human civilisation of all the forces contained in the animal world."[38]

In the midst of all the historical agonies of the mid-twentieth century, Teilhard affirmed an "absolute optimism" and foresaw "a spiritual renovation of the earth."[39] Man, he believed, is irreplaceable in the movement of the earth toward "irreversible perfection."[40] "The only universe capable of containing the human person is an irreversibly 'personalising' universe."[41] On scientific grounds the final success of hominisation is not certain, even though the process tends to "infallibilise" itself; for Christian faith success is "positively guaranteed by . . . God incarnate in his creation."[42]

Teilhard's writings mingle science (including unverifiable extrapolations from limited data), speculative metaphysics, and poetic imagination. Hence his influence, intoxicating to some, is baffling to others. His attraction has been less in his conclusions, which few accept without

qualifications, than in his eagerness to welcome evolutionary science, his zest for the future, and his dynamism
within an ecclesiasticism that has too often suffered from
rigidity.

If Teilhard's humanism is extravagant, Vatican II estab-
lished a more moderate humanism as normative for Ca-
tholicism. Significantly, Jacques Maritain appeared at the
Council on its final day and was acknowledged by Pope
Paul VI. A day earlier the pope had officially promulgated
one of the major documents of the Council, the *Pastoral
Constitution on the Church in the Modern World* (*Gau-
dium et Spes*). Building on the earlier encyclicals of Pope
John XXIII, *Mater et Magistra* and *Pacem in Terris*, the
Council declared its humanistic concern unmistakably.

The Fathers warned, to be sure, against "a humanism
which is merely earth-bound" (par. 56), and they observed:
"Some laud man so extravagantly that their faith in God
lapses into a kind of anemia" (par. 19). But they began by
declaring that "nothing genuinely human fails to raise an
echo" in the hearts of followers of Christ (par. 1). They
pointed to the "supremely human character of the mission
of the Church" (par. 11) and said, "Christians cannot
yearn for anything more ardently than to serve the men
of the modern world ever more generously and effectively" (par. 93). They affirmed "reverence for man" (par.
27), the desire for "an authentic and full humanity" of
every man (par. 53), the quest for "a world more genuinely human" (par. 77) and more suited to "man's sur-
passing dignity" (par. 91). Because the document pointed
so plainly to the rampant forces destructive of humanity
in the world, it was the more impressive when it affirmed,
"This sacred Synod proclaims the highest destiny of man
and champions the godlike seed which has been sown in
him" (par. 3).

Pope Paul reaffirmed this Catholic humanism in his Easter encyclical (March 26, 1967), *On the Development of Peoples (Populorum Progressio)*. The vocabulary is unmistakable, as it refers to "a transcendent humanism," "a new humanism," a "complete humanism," a "true humanism," a "universal humanism" (see pars. 16, 20, 42, 72). The church, wrote Paul, holds up "a global vision of man and of the human race" (par. 13). In God's design "each man can grow in humanity, can enhance his personal worth, can become more a person" (par. 15). But this is possible only with "the simultaneous development of all humanity in the spirit of solidarity" (par. 43). So he asked for "a world where every man, no matter what his race, religion or nationality, can live a fully human life" (par. 47).

Contemporary Catholicism, celebrating *aggiornamento,* has made clear its Christian humanistic commitment. Through both its individual theologians and its official utterances it speaks clearly, and increasingly the non-Catholic world listens.

CHAPTER V

The Celebration of the Secular

One aspect of the new humanism is its profound appreciation for the secular—that is, an appreciation for the history in which we live as a realm of real possibilities and opportunities, not simply as a meaningless process or a preparation for a life to come. The ethos is that of a rejoicing in this world rather than a resigned endurance. It means an awareness that in the nitty-gritty of life, in the struggles, the triumphs, the disappointments of existence, we seek and discover our destiny. Man's economic, political, and aesthetic ventures are expressions of his humanity.

Behind this celebration of the secular is a long history of the emancipation of man from the domination of heteronomous authority—of Scriptures, priesthoods, sacred kingships, and cults that imposed commands and prescribed obedience. The Renaissance, the Enlightenment, the romantic movement, the industrial revolution, and more recently the anticolonial and racial revolutions all mark stages in this victory of freedom. They are the *Heilsgeschichte,* the salvation-history of the secular spirit.

To the traditionalist and the devout this history has sometimes seemed irreverent and profane. It has repre-

sented the crude shouldering aside or the blasé ignoring
of God. But the new humanism, rather than fearing the
secular, embraces it. It erects no walls around the fortress
of faith; it sallies forth into the secular to find there its
home. It exults in human nature and in potentialities
released from traditional inhibitions. It becomes aware of
God and aims to serve God among men.

Such a drive in the church is, of course, not entirely
new. But, whatever its antecedents through the centuries,
it took new forms in modern history. And, to recall again
Paul Tillich's comment,[1] the history of Christian thought
in the last two centuries has been the drama of collision
and synthesis between the classical tradition and the rising
humanism.

Only a generation ago the social gospel called the church
to involvement in the struggles of industrial society and
insisted that Christian faithfulness found its milieu as
truly in the secular as in the ecclesiastical world. At the
Oxford Conference of 1937, Reinhold Niebuhr asserted
that Christian theology must acknowledge "gratitude to
the forces of modern secularism" for their passion for
justice and freedom and their objection to pretensions of
sanctity in church and civilization. "A warfare against
God," he said, "may be prompted by a prophetic passion
for God and scorn for the dubious political divinities
which seek to borrow His holiness."[2]

The years that immediately followed, however, did not
make it easy to appreciate the progress of secular history.
Christians saw the need to distinguish their faith from the
idolatries of political tyranny, racialism, and economic
ideologies, whether communist or capitalist. Theology for
the most part emphasized the difference, sometimes the
opposition, between God and the world. The proclama-

tion of the Christian gospel in those years put far more emphasis on the forgiveness of sin than upon the evocation of the creative vitalities inherent in the nature of man.

It is all the more remarkable, then, that the most impressive exultancy in the secular came from a prisoner of the Nazis. To understand the new Christian appreciation of secular man, we must look again at the writings of Dietrich Bonhoeffer.

THE WORLDLY FAITH OF BONHOEFFER

The place to begin is two statements from Bonhoeffer, which I have already quoted earlier.

Jesus does not call men to a new religion, but to life.
The Christian is not a *homo religiosus*, but a man, pure and simple.[3]

Here is the welcoming of life in its fullness, an appreciation of our secular humanity. In understanding what is involved here, it is helpful to distinguish three motives in Bonhoeffer's drive toward the secular.

The first is his rejoicing in the powers of man. Some of his phrases have by this time unfortunately been made into a jargon: "a world . . . come of age," "the adulthood of the world," "the newly matured world."[4] Before gulping them too hastily into the theological maw, we need to examine them. We can put them beside the call of another notable humanist, Albert Camus, "to forsake our age and its adolescent furies."[5] Bonhoeffer in Tegel Prison knew something about the immaturity of man. What did he mean by "a world come of age"?

He was saying that man can take responsibility for himself and his world, no longer calling on God for many of the purposes for which his ancestors evoked the divine. This human achievement is both intellectual and practical; that is, man can explain the world and can do things without resorting to God. It is "wrong . . . to use God as a stop-gap for the incompleteness of our knowledge."[6] "Man has learned to cope with all questions of importance without recourse to God as a working hypothesis."[7]

Men used to use God or the gods to explain most things that happen; now they have found scientifically understandable causes. Of course, the religious can always point to some gaps in human knowledge. But this is a losing method. It means that God keeps retreating, eventually so far that he makes no difference. Instead of grudgingly yielding ground, step by step, to the advancing secular understanding, Christians should welcome it.

There is a sleazy apologetic, Bonhoeffer said, that tries to beat man down and drive him into misery—in order to come to his rescue with word of God. It tells happy men that they are wretched and it drives them to despair in order to save them. This tactic—"secularized methodism"[8]—is both ignoble and futile. Men come of age will not succumb to it.

Bonhoeffer's most dramatic statement is this: "God is teaching us that we must live as men who can get along very well without him."[9] The meaning of that sentence depends upon how we read it—on how we relate the message (getting along without God) to the one who teaches it (God). The "death of God" theologians have used the statement to claim Bonhoeffer for their cause. Bonhoeffer himself went on to write: "Nothing is impossible for all things are possible with God."[10] In prison he found himself sustained by "the prayers of others, both known and unknown."[11]

Whatever the ultimate meanings of Bonhoeffer's thinking, one immediate meaning is surely persuasive. Man has learned to do a lot. He can manage his world and his future as men could not in the past. He can irrigate his deserts rather than pray for rain, can vaccinate his children rather than beg God to spare them from smallpox, can increase food production and regulate population rather than await manna from heaven. Recognition and appreciation of these powers and responsibilities is part of the new humanism.

A second meaning in Bonhoeffer's impulse toward the secular is his decisive rejection of the temptation to confine faith to a religious ghetto. The temptation is real— the enemies of faith try to drive it and its friends try to lure it into isolation. Avoid politics, stick to spiritual values, stay out of controversy, live in your own cozy world—these are the slogans of the tempters. The new appreciation for the secular, like the ancient faith of the prophets, refuses such evasiveness.

One way of making the point is to call for a "religionless Christianity." I shall come back to this theme in Chapter XIV. For the moment it is enough to notice Bonhoeffer's desire to understand Christ, not as "the object of religion" but as "the Lord of the world."[12]

A third meaning in the welcoming of the secular is the orientation of faith to the present and the future. It is the rejection of the ideal of Christendom—of a stable society, of a patriarchal culture in which men are secure in their status and identity, of a theology in which God is the defender of the *status quo*. Secularization means the technological revolution and urbanization. It means a fluid society and a social order in which human relations are largely a matter of choice rather than the organized society in which relations are determined by kinship and geography.

Urbanization and technology substitute, in part, a man-made environment for a naturally given one. They surround man with evidences of his dominion rather than his creatureliness. In both the possibilities and frustrations of life, the human factors tend to obscure the natural. Man takes his clues more from man than from nature.

Bonhoeffer had a divided mind on this issue. He was perhaps the last great theologian who dared to avow a preference for the rural soil over the alluring brilliance of the city.[13] Today the theologian, aware of the disapproval of his peer group, does not venture such thoughts. Bonhoeffer did. But as he did, he looked for the opportunity in the future, even when it threatened the comfortable values of the past. So he wrote:

We may have to face events and changes which run counter to our rights and wishes. But if so, we shall not give way to bitterness and foolish pride, but consciously submit to divine judgment, and thus prove our worthiness to survive by identifying ourselves generously and unselfishly with the life of the community and the interests of our fellowmen.[14]

SECULARIZATION: THE BIBLE AND TODAY

The new appreciation of the secular comes, at least in part, from Biblical sources. Friedrich Gogarten developed this idea in an influential book of 1953, whose title might be translated, *Destiny and Hope of the Modern Age: Secularization as a Theological Problem.*[15] Gogarten argued that Biblical faith frees men from the domination of a totalitarian cosmos, in which the divinized forces of nature impose a pattern upon human life.

The prophetic faith of Scripture objects to the worship

of nature and the idols of nature. It asks man to make his decisions in response to a living God. Neither God nor man is bound within the cyclical patterns of nature.

A number of modern scientists and historians of science have suggested that Christianity, less by any conscious intention of Christians than by the implicit direction of their beliefs, has contributed to the rise of science and man's consequent expansion of powers. Nature, according to Christian faith, is the creation of God. Thus the natural order is freed from the taboos that forbid its scientific investigation in some religions; yet it is worthy of investigation, contrary to the teachings of religions that think of the physical world as evil or as unreal.[16]

In 1959 a consultation of university teachers at the Ecumenical Institute (Bossey, Switzerland) investigated "The Meaning of the Secular."[17] The meeting was well timed both to scrutinize a concern of the hour and to stimulate further thinking on the subject. The next few years saw a variety of writings that developed the idea that modern secularization is in some authentic sense a consequence rather than an enemy of Christian faith.

The expressions of the new "Christian worldliness" come in great variety, but share a commitment both to Biblical faith and to the world today. J. C. Hoekendijk unites the double concern in these sentences: "The kerygma of the early Christians did not know of a redemptive act of God that was not directed toward the whole world. . . . As Christians we have our *Sitz im Leben* (life situation) *in the world,* not in the church."[18]

Paul van Buren seeks not a secular alternative to the gospel but "the secular meaning of the gospel."[19] Harvey Cox sees secularization as "the legitimate consequence of the impact of biblical faith on history."[20] Arend van Leeuwen regards secularization as "the creative and liberating activity of the Word of God."[21] Ronald Gregor Smith, in a book called *Secular Christianity,* writes: "Thus we may recognize Christ as the truly secular man, the one who lives entirely by faith, and thus entirely freely for the world, and entirely freely for God."[22]

In such expressions we do not have a cavalier secularization in which men so love the world that they would rather not be bothered by God. We have a recognition that Christian faith lives itself out in the world of men and is concerned for men. H. D. Wendland made the point forcefully in one of the Geneva documents. The work of the church is not to develop an "ethic for Christians." Rather, the church is "the advocate of *humanitas,*" engaged in "love's secular action." Thus, he continued, "Agape gives help by using every human, secular (for example, technical and scientific) means in every imaginable form of social assistance."[23]

The new celebration of the secular may be both Christian and humanistic. Hoekendijk describes God as "that incorrigible Humanist"[24]—thereby reminding the church that faith's response to God is a concern for men. At the same time some of the new humanists warn that secularization has also its destructive possibilities. M. M. Thomas, while praising van Leeuwen's book, *Christianity in World History,* criticizes it on one major issue. Van Leeuwen, says Thomas, "seems blind to the seriousness of the dehumanising trends at the heart of western culture, which erupted only the other day in modern revival of pagan demons and gods in Nazism and still finds expression in Western ethos."[25]

The appropriate warning comes from the pioneer theological leader of the new humanism. Dietrich Bonhoeffer once studied in the United States during an earlier era of enthusiastic secularization. Then (1930–1931) he warned that the theological atmosphere—he referred specifically to Union Theological Seminary—was "accelerating the process of the secularisation of Christianity in America." In part this process was a "healthy and necessary" criticism of fundamentalism. "But," he wrote, "there is no sound basis on which one can rebuild after demolition. It is carried away with the general collapse."[26]

In some ways Bonhoeffer changed his mind when he became a celebrant of secularization. But not entirely. In his discovery of the "worldliness" of Christianity, he said:

I don't mean the shallow this-worldliness of the enlightened, of the busy, the comfortable or the lascivious. It's something much more profound than that, something in which the knowledge of death and resurrection is ever present.[27]

Such a warning chastens without smothering the current zest for the secular. It is not simply an effort to outdo the world on its own terms, singing, "Anything you can do we can do better." It enters fully into human life, bringing to that life a judging and healing word from the gospel.

The new humanism sees well that much Christian hostility to the world has actually been only a longing for a comfortable tradition—a Christian version of the flesh-pots of Egypt. So it wisely warns against confinement in the categorical cell of "Christ against culture." At its best it is equally aware of the prison of the "Christ of culture."[28]

CHAPTER VI

Uneasiness in the Brave New World

Within the new humanism lurk deep uncertainties and fears. As Roger Mehl, the French philosopher, has put it: "Our age has a concern and even an obsession with *man*. However, this does not hinder it from being a hard and cruel age for man."[1]

In objective terms, everybody has become familiar with the problem. President Kennedy stated it plainly in his inaugural address: "For man holds in his mortal hands the power to abolish all forms of human poverty and all forms of human life." But in this book I am concerned less with the vast social problem of our time than with the human nature that lives in and with the social problems. Man is the live, conscious, trembling seismograph who responds to the reverberations of history. He is also, though he sometimes doubts it, the initiator and director of the social changes that shape and disturb him.

Some years ago, in a comment on humorist James Thurber, Wolcott Gibbs said, "Thurber has a firm grasp on confusion." Perhaps Thurber was a man of the future. As the tempo and complexity of life increase, the only persons who can direct their course are those with a grasp of confusion—and perhaps something of a Thurberesque sense of humor about it.

The peculiar problem of our age is that the same achievements that have led man to exult in his own powers have also threatened his personal being and integrity. The science that elevates man's capacities also degrades him by turning him into an object for research and manipulation. The industrial technology that raises the standard of living (for the affluent minority of the world) also seems increasingly to make men unnecessary.

Bertrand Russell has asked the question, "Has man a future?" "He has survived, hitherto, through ignorance. Can he continue to survive now that the useful degree of ignorance is lost? . . . Can *scientific* man survive?"[2] Russell advocates an affirmative answer, but he is not sure that history will vindicate his hope.

The new humanism is challenged by the many dehumanizing forces in our world. This chapter deals with three of the inner questions and conflicts that haunt man and influence his understanding of himself: his search for identity, his struggle with alienation, and his quest for meaning.

THE SEARCH FOR IDENTITY

To be a person is to know oneself and others, to recognize oneself and friends as unique and irreplaceable. It is to have and to know an identity, to recognize identities in others.

In traditionally organized societies, personal identity is conferred upon the individual. A man may be known by his home and family. In the New Testament, Jesus was identified as the man of Nazareth, the carpenter's son; he caused wonder and perplexity when he stepped outside that given identity. Insofar as society confers identity upon a person, he need not constantly identify himself— to strangers or himself. They and he know who he is.

In mobile industrial societies identity is no longer conferred; it must be discovered or created. Youth, in particular, asks the question, "Who am I?" One of the most frequent reasons given by students for entering college or for dropping out, for serving a hitch in the army or for joining a protest movement, is to discover their identity.

In many ways the changing situation is a humanistic gain. To discover and choose one's identity, rather than simply to accept a conferred identity, is a mark of freedom. Many a young person, facing a career, is no longer limited, as were his parents or grandparents, to doing a laborer's work, a woman's work, a Negro's work.

But a society where identity is up for grabs also produces confusion. The abandonment of traditional male and female roles means both liberation and confusion in sexual identity. Ethnic identity becomes increasingly perplexing; many a Negro is unsure whether he wants to escape or to acclaim his racial heritage, and many a WASP (white Anglo-Saxon Protestant), whose parents took their identity for granted, is himself perplexed and guilt-ridden in this identity. The youth culture, which once sought to submerge its identity in an eagerness to become adult, now asserts its identity in protest against the culture of the establishment. The confusion of values and self-identification sometimes pushes people to the edge of personal and social pathologies.[3]

In several ways contemporary society sets obstacles before the person seeking identity. In doing so, it forces people to rethink the issue of what it is to be human.

One such obstacle is the deliberate effort to make individuals expendable. The military organization is the best example of a system constructed on the assumption of expendability. Casualties are part of the way of life in combat, and the organization must go on, no matter what persons are lost. In many ways society is becoming more like the army. The assembly line and the coded job description are designed to employ replaceable skills rather than irreplaceable persons. For most purposes anonymity becomes an asset to the system.

In a modern city, unlike a tribal society, everybody is anonymous in many of his activities. Such anonymity need not be personally destructive; for many purposes it has advantages. But nobody can be anonymous all the time. When he becomes anonymous to his friends and to himself, he has ceased to be sane and human.

A second obstacle to identity is the changed meaning of work. One way in which man has known himself has been as a producer and a worker. We need not romanticize the historical meaning of work, which has often been an impersonal drudgery or an imposed task for the benefit of somebody other than the worker. But in work man has usually known that he was needed, and he has sometimes had the satisfaction of being a creator.

Now those satisfactions are eroding for many people. Some workers are learning that they are less useful and more troublesome than the machines that replace them. Society can discover—and with moderate good sense can learn to implement—social mechanisms to deal with the problems of employment and income. It will have more trouble rethinking the human meaning of work. To do so may be a rewarding experience. But at the moment it is a disconcerting one. And it has a destructive effect upon the identity of some persons.

A third obstacle to identity is the increased necessity of coordination and social controls in a huge technological society. As populations explode and various cultures and subcultures become increasingly interdependent, life becomes related to life in impersonal ways. The processes of survival have to keep going. The activities of every person and group fit into wider contexts that he does not understand. Economically, politically, and culturally the person is part of an intricate network that includes thousands and millions of people whom he does not know. Somebody, many somebodies, are always trying to control the network from open or hidden centers of power.

The resulting uneasiness has found expression in the anti-utopias of modern literature—for example, Orwell's *Nineteen Eighty-Four* and Huxley's *Brave New World*.[4] Twenty-six years after the fictional *Brave New World*, Huxley published a book of essays called *Brave New World Revisited*.[5] In it he declared himself "less optimistic" than in the earlier book, because his prophecies were coming true much faster than he had expected. He also offered some solutions that, to many readers, looked disturbingly like his most foreboding predictions.

In past societies man has, no doubt, been too prone to find his identity in a narrow provincialism. To rediscover his identity in a global world, where his good is related to the good of everyone, can mark an advance in realism and imagination. The change brings what Kenneth Boulding calls "the greatest dilemma of the twentieth century": "If the great transition is to be achieved without destroying man's sense of his own importance, dignity, and community, and these three things go strongly together, there must be strong local and traditional subcultures to provide the intimacy, the deep personal relationships, and the identity with a small manageable community which the world superculture cannot provide."[6]

A fourth obstacle—implicit in the three already mentioned—is the tendency to regard man as a thing rather than a person, not only in certain external ways but in his deepest selfhood. In his economic life (both as producer and consumer) and his political life, man senses that he is regarded as a manipulable object. Some of the new sciences of behavior increasingly regard him as such. After a while, man starts thinking of himself as an object. Then he is likely to face a real crisis of identity.

Perhaps the best example is the meaning of sexuality. On the obvious level the publicized "sexual revolution" means the freeing of sexuality, due to contraceptives and changing moral codes and attitudes, from some traditional restraints and inhibitions. What may be more significant is the tendency to detach sexuality from personal identity. The belief that the sexual relation is an intimately human relationship of personal love has been a notable and precarious achievement of man. It can be lost in the idea that sexual practices are impersonal processes requiring no real involvement of the self.

A reviewer of the play *The Deer Park* writes: "Eitel and Elena, after the modern convention, exchange avowals of the amplitude of their sexual responses rather than saying, as heroes and heroines used to do, that they love each other."[7] We might ask whether a love story like Ernest Hemingway's *Farewell to Arms* (1929) now belongs to a dated past. I mention that particular novel, not to idealize it—the affair was extramarital and in certain other respects irresponsible—but because it may go down in history as one of the last stories of ardent love. Conceivably the next generation, with tastes adjusted to what Mary McCarthy calls "a pepless *Playboy* flavor," may read it (if at all) with a curious wonder and maybe a little envy. And the love and jealousy of Shakespeare's *Othello* may become a bit of data for cultural anthropology, about as remote from our society as the rain dances of the Zuñi Indians.

Rollo May reports that the psychotherapist's patients rarely seek help for the old problems of guilt and inhibition connected with sex. Instead they complain of disappointment in the sexual experience. Sex does not live up to the promises. It lacks the personal vitality and meaning that people had been led to expect. Something powerful and personal is missing.[8]

Sexuality, of course, is only one quality, although a fundamental one, of selfhood. It is one of the many evidences of the crisis of personal identity in the evolving society.

THE STRUGGLE WITH ALIENATION

The other side of identity is alienation. Sometimes the person with a strong sense of personal identity—for example, the prophet, whose identity is connected with his calling—can risk social alienation. But personal identity is always, in part, a participation in a meaningful heritage and community. Hence, alienation and loss of identity usually go together.

It is rather suddenly that alienation has become one of the *au courant* words of our time, part of the going vocabulary of Marxists, theologians, psychologists, the New Left, and almost everyone who tries to analyze contemporary society. At first glance it may seem to represent a new phenomenon. Not long ago the great complaint about American culture was centered on conformity. David Riesman described the "other-directed" character type who guided his actions and even his feelings by a psychic radar that gave him signals from the people around him.[9] William H. Whyte, Jr., described the "organization man," who had submerged himself and the traditional "Protestant ethic" in the world of the corporation and the corporation-style suburb.[10] As recently as 1957, sociologist Philip Jacob's study of American college students described them as "gloriously contented" and "dutifully responsive toward government."[11]

But there were other signs, including talk of a beat generation and disaffiliated youth. In the same year that Philip Jacob published his findings, Kenneth Rexroth wrote: "The youngest generation is in a state of revolt so absolute that its elders cannot even recognize it. The disaffiliation, alienation, and rejection of the young has, as far as their elders are concerned, moved out of the visible spectrum altogether."[12] A few years later the revolt had become highly visible. In southern towns where college students joined the Negro freedom movement and at Berkeley and many another campus, young people gave public notice of their discontents. Alienation, not conformity, was the great issue.

What happened? Was there a sudden reversal from conformity to rebellion? Probably not. Alienated people may find in conformity a pseudoanswer to their craving for something more humanly authentic. If "the system"—including the dominant values and institutions of a society—smothers men's deepest aspirations and discontents under a blanket of affluent efficiency, those who live in it may cling all the more desperately to the system, not because they love it but because it is all they have. As Herbert Marcuse puts it in *One Dimensional Man*, "the subject which is alienated is swallowed up by its alienated existence."[13] That is, the person, alienated from others and from his own most personal being, may act out his anxieties by seeking security and meaning in the only available ways. But he knows or half knows the shallow-

ness of his pseudofaith, and someday he—or his children
—may rebel.

It is obviously among youth that alienation expresses itself most openly. Youth have not yet committed themselves so thoroughly as adults to the going ways. They are
not yet hostages of the system with its rituals, its loyalties,
and its morals. Many of them know what Paul Goodman
means by "growing up absurd."[14] They have grown up in
an age "not of commitment but of alienation," an age in
which "many Americans are left with an inarticulate sense
of loss, of unrelatedness and lack of connection"—to use
the description of Kenneth Keniston.[15]

Of course, youth is as capable of posturing as any other
group in our society. And there is considerable posturing
among those who insist, "You can't trust anybody over
thirty." No segment of society, including even youth, is
entirely trustworthy—or free from the uneasiness that ac-
companies the new humanism.

Youth, if that term has any collective meaning, is in
almost as much disarray as the rest of the world. It includes the "mystical militants" of the New Left, Michael
Harrington's term to describe the most articulate and
idealistic of our youth.[16] It includes the international subculture of the beatniks and the hippies, who are as uninterested in the new politics as in the old, who have fled
from the world of public affairs to their more personal
visions, sometimes stimulated by LSD.[17] It includes the
increasingly sullen and resentful victims of racial prejudice. It includes those defined by society as delinquents;
one out of six boys in the United States is referred to
juvenile court.[18] It includes those for whom alienation is
a status symbol and a new form of conformity to the peer
group. And it includes the majority of conservative youth

whose aim is to achieve a life approximately like and a little more affluent than that of their parents—but with an undertone of mockery of the whole system that their parents do not quite understand.

The adult world is half resentful of youth for failing to appreciate what an older generation is passing on to its children. It is half envious of youth for revealing the stress and distress that a more tired generation usually represses.

The problem of alienation is summed up, about as briefly as possible, in two short sentences from two playwrights who have addressed our time. The first is Jean-Paul Sartre, who created a character who said, "Hell is—other people."[19] The other is T. S. Eliot, whose character a little later said, "Hell is oneself."[20] The two statements just about exhaust the possibilities—unless perhaps some metaphysical alienation underlies and infuses man's discontents both with other people and with himself.

THE QUEST FOR MEANING

Inseparable from the problems of identity and of alienation is the question of meaning. Paul Tillich's description of the rise of modern humanism, which we have already noticed, belongs in the context of his historical analysis of anxiety. In *The Courage to Be* he pointed to three characteristic types of anxiety. Ancient man knew the anxiety of fate and death; for medieval man it was the anxiety of guilt and condemnation. Modern man experiences the anxiety of meaninglessness.[21]

H. Richard Niebuhr confirmed this judgment of contemporary man:

Our situation is not one of conflict between great forces. It is better described as a situation of emptiness. Life for man has become empty because it is without great purposes and great hopes and great commitments, without a sense of participation in a great conflict of good and evil.[22]

The point is not that there are no great evils to oppose, no goals to realize. It is that, for reasons hard to understand, our culture perceives "the banality of evil" more than its "diabolical or demonic profundity," to use Hannah Arendt's phrases.[23] And the new humanism is far more confident of its means than of its purposes.

For a brief time in the 1960's the civil rights movement stirred many Americans to participation in meaningful conflict where great issues were at stake and human action made a difference. But the classical period of that struggle quickly passed. The problem remains, no less a burden on the conscience of America and no less a call to creative, healing activity. But soon the concentration of society turned to the far less inspiring war in Vietnam. The civil rights cause—if I may point simply to its mood rather than make any moral judgment upon it—became a grinding, frustrating burden among divided partisans against forces of invisible inertia and resistance.

It may be that such struggles—rather than dramatic, exhilarating conflicts—are typical of the human situation. It may be that what man needs to learn is that the meaning of his life usually lies half-hidden among many partial and questionable meanings rather than identified by trumpets and pennants. If so, those data are an important part of the human condition and the recognition of valid human purposes in a perplexing world.

A decade ago Carl Sandburg, who as a younger man had celebrated the vitality of Chicago, returned to that city for a "Chicago dynamic" celebration, sponsored—characteristically in our society, I am tempted to say—by Chicago steel makers. Sandburg once again tried his poetic eloquence on the urban scene:

> When one tall skyscraper is torn down
> To make room for a taller one to go up
> Who takes down and puts up those skyscrapers?
> Man—the little two-legged joker . . . MAN.[24]

The words try to reaffirm the dignity and creativity of man in a world where his own technological works often dwarf him. They are accurate in pointing out that man is not a mere midget, lost in the skyscraper jungle, but the maker of the buildings. Yet they say nothing of the meaning of all this human activity. What is the point of taking down skyscrapers to put up taller ones? The question of meaning leaps persistently out of the tribute to man.

We must return to this theme later. It is the most urgent and most persistent issue in man's effort at self-understanding. For the moment it must suffice to say that the celebration of humanity, so prominent in the new humanism, is a lyric obbligato over chords that express deep unease about the being and destiny of modern man.

PART TWO

The Progress of Some Critical Dialogues

CHAPTER VII

The Importance of Dialogue

Humanism is interested in the whole range of human experience. Hence it is likely to appropriate any insights it can find into the condition of man. This interest in all that man learns and does influences the method of the theologies that are developing the new humanism.

I must quickly grant that there is no single theological method. Karl Barth has shown that a theology of the Word of God, a theology taking its sources strictly from Biblical revelation, can be decisively humanistic. But the new humanism, in its theological developments, is more likely to use a method like that of Paul Tillich, who takes his sources from all realms of human experience, interpreting them in the light of a norm from Scripture.

In any such method the dialogue of theology with other disciplines becomes important. Theology wants to know what man is learning about man in the sciences, what he is saying and revealing of himself in the arts. It enters into dialogue, both to listen and to talk. It expects to learn from the dialogue and contribute to it.

This book, from the beginning, has assumed the importance of such dialogue. Although the book is about Christian doctrine, I have reported information and ideas from many people who do not consider themselves theologians or Christians. Such people, nevertheless, are contributing to the Christian doctrine of man.

When theology enters into interdisciplinary dialogue, it cannot predetermine the outcome. To enter interdisciplinary conversations, aiming to pick up a little reinforcement and neglect any possible refutation, is to enter a pseudodialogue. Even so, the history of genuine dialogues suggests certain expectations that are appropriate.

Theologians should not expect representatives of other disciplines to talk like theologians and, above all, should not evaluate them on the basis of similarities in vocabulary. Scientists and philosophers, if they are doing their job well, are likely to say things about man that the theologian does not usually say and perhaps never even thinks of saying. There would be no point in having a variety of intellectual disciplines and methods if all were doing the same thing.

On the other hand, if all the disciplines are studying the same human subject, they must take account of each other. No one has a right to say, "Such and such ideas may be true for psychology or philosophy, but they are not true for theology." If they are true for psychology or philosophy, we must ask what they *mean* for theology.

In dialogue we must look rigorously for agreements or clashes, without jumping too quickly to conclusions. Seeming disagreements are often more helpful than seeming but deceptive agreements. The theologian will not get much help from the scientist or philosopher who trims his argument in order to be friendly to religion. The tough-minded scientist, more than the tender-minded one, often turns out to be the disturbing ally of a tough-minded faith.

The theologian, when he encounters a real difference, must inquire carefully into its nature. He may find any of three kinds of difference.

The first is a difference of perspective. For example, theology has traditionally said that God created men. Evolutionary science says that men are descendants of higher apes. Contemporary theology usually finds valid meaning in both statements. It understands both as meaningful statements within their own perspectives, and it assumes that an adequate view of man must take account of both perspectives.

The second is a direct clash of judgments. For example, there was a time when most theologians (and most scientists, for that matter) thought that the human race was only a few thousand years old. Then a newer science found evidence that man had inhabited the earth for hundreds of thousands of years. Obviously, both propositions could not be true. Theology and the older science wisely revised their formulations to take account of the new evidence. Such revision need cause no embarrassment at all, if the aim of theology is truth.

The third difference involves a clash of judgments that is not so easily resolved. For example, theology holds that man is in some significant sense a free and responsible being. Some scientists give a deterministic account of man as an automaton. Here theology will not quickly deny its insight to agree with the opposition. It will ask whether the scientist in the case is using determinism as a working hypothesis for the sake of limited operational procedures or whether he is basing an ontological conclusion on limited empirical evidence. If either is the situation, the theologian will not be intimidated. He will be radically prepared to confront any genuine evidence. But he will sometimes find that statements of specific scientists are not scientific conclusions but faith statements; and when it comes to faith statements, the theologian will exercise his own competence in evaluating them.

Part Two of this book looks into five important dialogues of theology: with the biological sciences, with psychology, with some of the social sciences, with existentialism, and with Marxism. In selecting these five, I must omit others that are just as important. Furthermore, it will quickly be evident that within each of the five I am considering only a small selection from the available evidence. The purpose of this section is to give a sampling, not a summary. The samples provide some concrete evidence of the way in which the dialogue with other disciplines influences theology.

CHAPTER VIII

Questions from the New Biology

Biology, the science of life, tells us about ourselves as living organisms. What it tells us is often astonishing—increasingly so, for biology is moving fast. Kenneth Boulding in *The Meaning of the Twentieth Century* suggests that "we are now on the edge of a biological revolution which may have results for mankind just as dramatic as the nuclear revolution of a generation ago."[1]

The impact of biology on society is most evident in medicine. Even the least scientific people are aware of organ transplants, "miracle medicines," and the remarkable powers of many new kinds of pills, including, of course, "the pill."

Especially important for the understanding of the nature of man is the group of psychopharmaceutical drugs. Among these are the tranquilizers (or psychohibitors) so widely used to calm people down in a high-tension world. There are the stimulants (or psychoactivators), which increase wakefulness and intensify psychic functions. There are the antidepressants, which may produce euphoria or combat severe depression in mental patients. And there are the increasingly notable (or notorious) drugs such as LSD, which either produce abnormal psychic states or remove the inhibitions that normally limit human awareness.[2]

Even more "far out" than such drugs, which are actually in use, are the discoveries on the relation between chemistry and memory. That there is some relation between RNA (ribonucleic acid) molecules and memory is well established, but the exact relation is not certain. Experiments with flatworms seemed to open up unexpected possibilities. A group of worms learned to respond to electric light and shock. Then some of their RNA cells were transferred (both by digestion and by injection) into untrained worms, who apparently thus acquired the knowledge that their predecessors had learned. One prompt result was some new proposals for human education—that students might learn by eating their teachers. However, eighteen experiments in eight different laboratories failed to produce any comparable transfer of learning in rats, who are presumably more like man than the flatworms—and the teaching profession relaxed.[3]

The humanistic significance of all these developments is in the evidence that chemicals are effective, to some unknown extent, in modifying human qualities that are often ascribed to the mind or the spirit. A different line of experimentation works on the same issue through the electronic processes in the brain. Experiments have located the specific centers in the brain that direct certain biological and psychic functions. Electric stimulation of those centers can influence and change behavior.

Dr. José M. R. Delgado, of the Yale Medical School, has implanted electrodes in the brains of animals, then radioed signals that radically changed the animals' behavior. By such methods he has caused a monkey to exercise or abdicate his leader's role within a group of monkeys. He has influenced an affectionate female monkey to neglect her child, then (on removal of the electrical stimulus) to resume her motherly care. He has stopped a charging bull and sent it strolling away. Dr. Delgado insists that his demonstrations do not show that a man is a robot or that the experimenter can change the basic characteristics of a person or animal. But they do show the intimate relation between electronic and behavioral aspects of animal (and presumably human) life.[4]

One other branch of biological research raises the same issues. This is the study of molecular biology by biochemists who show the effect of man's interior chemistry upon his nature. Some of their most spectacular hypotheses emerge in investigation of heredity and proposals for eugenics. The mechanism of heredity operates through the DNA (deoxyribonucleic acid) molecules in the genes. The processes are incredibly intricate, but recent years have brought spectacular advances in the understanding of them. For example, the genetic causes and modes of transmission of certain hereditary diseases are now fairly well known.

One consequence of the new information is the fervent crusade of some scientists for "positive eugenics." (Positive eugenics is the eugenic improvement of the human race, as contrasted with "negative eugenics," which is the more modest effort to prevent the transmission of specific hereditary diseases.) The proposals take two major forms.

The first was advanced most energetically by the late Hermann J. Muller, a Nobel laureate and pioneer in genetic studies. He recommended establishment of sperm banks, for the maintenance in a frozen state of the semen of distinguished men. Then through artificial insemination these men could become the genetic fathers of many persons. Muller believed that idealistic married couples would welcome the opportunity to rear the superior child who would come from such a process.[5]

The other method is sometimes called genetic surgery. It involves the synthesizing or modifying of the germinal cells, so that possibly through a chemical injection or some laboratory method the genes may be changed in desired ways. The popular literature on the subject projects a day when parents may set the specifications of beauty, brains, temperament, and physique for their offspring, then visit the doctor who would enable them to achieve the desired product. The scientific literature is more restrained.

Such prospects raise grave, even terrifying, ethical questions. Should the people of this generation have the right to inflict their ideal of man on the future, not merely by indoctrination and training, as they do now, but by determining the genetic constitution of generations to come? Will there be a genetic race, comparable to the armaments race, as nations compete to develop superwarriors for the future? Who will control the portentous process? As Theodosius Dobzhansky asks: "Are we to have, in place of Plato's philosopher-king, a geneticist-king? And who will be president of the National Sperm Bank and of the National DNA Bank?"[6]

All these recent developments in biology and genetics have some import for our understanding of the nature of man. The various examples I have used—psychopharmaceutical drugs, electronic control of the brain, and molecular genetics—raise the same question. Is man a physical-chemical mechanism? Are his cherished freedom, his personal character, his power to act for purposes all illusory? Or is there something dehumanizing in the hypothesis that chemical and electronic processes actually impose the actions that we think are human decisions?

To a point—a point hard to define—the new scientific judgments are congenial to traditional Christian faith. Theology commonly insists that the Bible sees man as a psychosomatic unity, a being who thinks with his heart and feels with his bowels, not as an arbitrary assembly of two disparate items, soul and body, as Plato sometimes and Descartes generally said. No one influenced by Biblical thought is surprised to hear that all kinds of biological processes enter into man's thinking and feeling.

But Christian doctrine has never asserted a materialistic behaviorism that reduces man to an object. That the self involves mechanisms is obvious; to say that the self is a mechanism is something else. Biblical anthropology has always discerned a transcendence in man, an ability to make decisions, a responsibility for his own actions that we cannot ascribe to chemical reactions or to electronic machines.

Human insight in the inherited wisdom of the race has always seen this point in one way or another. Winston Churchill voiced it in his tribute to Harry Hopkins:

His was a soul that flamed out of a frail and failing body. He was a crumbling lighthouse from which there shone the beams that led great fleets to harbour. . . . There he sat, slim, frail, ill, but absolutely glowing with refined comprehension of the Cause. . . . His love for the causes of the weak and poor was matched by his passion against tyranny, especially when tyranny was, for the time, triumphant.[7]

Anybody can understand what Churchill means by that contrast between soul and body. We might answer that the word "soul" has no scientific status and that DNA, RNA, and electronic impulses were part of everything that Harry Hopkins did or that Winston Churchill wrote in those sentences. True. But nothing in our analysis is any more real than the eloquence of Churchill or the resolution of the frail man whom he appreciated. If we are to be empirical, courage and responsible decision are as ineradicably part of the evidence as the hypotheses by which we make efforts at some understanding of human nature.

There remain many paradoxes in the relation between man and nature—or between man's personal self-understanding and the understanding he gets through the biological sciences. At the same time there are clues to living with those paradoxes. One clue comes from the changing understanding of nature. The more thoroughly we understand the workings of nature in man, the more we realize that we cannot understand nature solely in terms of its nonhuman aspects. If thought, anticipation, and decision are physical-chemical processes, then we need to revise some of the classical concepts of physics and chemistry. Physics itself keeps finding the nature of matter to be more mysterious and less "materialistic"—in the sense of the old concepts of inert stuff. Biology gives amazing descriptions of the activity within protoplasmic matter.

The amount of information contained in the chromosomes of a single fertilized egg is equivalent to about a thousand printed volumes of books, each as large as a volume of the *Encyclopaedia Britannica*. This amount of coded instruction packed into the size of a millionth of a pinhead is the remarkable material which transmits information from parent to offspring to tell the next generation how to make a person.[8]

When scientists talk about matter transmitting information and telling other matter what to do—even with all due allowances for metaphors—they are no longer talking about the world machine of classical physics. Kenneth Boulding, economist and social philosopher, looking at the results of the physical and biological sciences, says:

All change is fundamentally a change in the system of information and knowledge. . . . We now know that the gene acts as a printer, that it imprints its own pattern on the matter around it, and hence is able to multiply its own structure many billion times.
In the beginning, indeed, is always the Word. The seed of anything, of a man, of a nation, of a church, of a society, or of a whole new world, is always a body of coded information.[9]

To whatever extent man is a material being, he requires us to ascribe to matter remarkable qualities. Matter then becomes capable of planning and seeking goals, of courage, of self-sacrifice, of visions (illusory or genuine), of seeking truth.

But it is only living matter that does all these things. So biologist Edmund Sinnott says, "Protoplasm is a bridge between atoms, on the one hand, and the flowering of the spirit on the other."[10] He shows that the living organism behaves very differently from the corpse, even though they may be separated only by a moment and the actual chemical ingredients are almost identical. A bit of matter—say, some food—behaves differently when ingested into the organism from the way it behaves outside the organism. The organism has the ability to maintain its identity, even though there is a constant turnover of matter within it, as matter constantly enters and leaves the system.[11] Even more remarkable, the life processes appear to buck the prevailing trend of the physical universe. Entropy (the process described by the second law of thermodynamics) means that in general matter and energy move toward disorder, toward chaos, toward a "running down of the system." But life, both in the evolutionary process and in the single organism, organizes matter in elaborate systems and moves toward higher organization.[12]

Of all living organisms, man is both the most intricate and the one we human beings know most directly. Whatever his internal chemistry or electronic functions, man is still that mysterious being, a part of nature who can reflect about nature and himself, who can pursue goals, distinguish alternatives, make decisions, and ask questions about his own nature. Nowhere is this more evident than in the current thinking of biologists themselves. The enthusiastic geneticist, for example, sometimes seems to assume that the human character is the direct result of genetic chemistry and that the manipulation of DNA can produce any wanted type of person. But the same geneticist assumes that *he*—the geneticist—can exercise rational wisdom and freedom in prescribing the type of character who should be produced. He never writes as though a purely mechanical process of DNA chemistry within the present generation were determining the character of the future. He seeks to persuade; he writes of ideals; he thinks as a person addressing other persons. He takes for granted a *human* validity in his own thinking that cannot be ascribed to impersonal biological chemistry alone.

Thus Hermann Muller wished to use genetic methods to increase "brotherly love" and "deep and broad warm-heartedness," combined with initiative and aggressiveness in the sense of "independence of judgment and moral courage." Yet he feared that the "raucous, hypocritical" values of contemporary culture might direct genetic efforts in the wrong directions.[13] Obviously when he made his moral judgments, he did not regard himself, the judging person, as a mechanism whose operations were dictated by its own chemical processes. He assumed that he, as a person, was somehow capable of evaluating his own feelings and the attitudes of his society.

Experimentation with rats has shown the possibility of breeding strains with a high level of innate aggressiveness or passivity. Occasionally somebody therefore assumes that a scientifically heroic effort might breed human beings with the ideal combination of independence and love. But aggressiveness is not independence, and passivity is not love. Human character depends upon the human use of given impulses.

Some biologists have unabashedly acknowledged this quality of transcendence in human personality. Thus geneticist Theodosius Dobzhansky writes:

Natural selection has not propagated genes for ethics, or genes for inventing Euclidean geometry, propounding evolutionary theories, composing musical symphonies, painting landscapes, making a million dollars on Wall Street, loving the soil, or becoming a military leader. Such genes simply do not exist.[14]

Microbiologist Catherine Roberts is even more emphatic. Replying to Julian Huxley's idea that genetics might produce "more and better saints and moral leaders," she says: "I would say that positive eugenicists, despite their earnest intentions, know nothing—absolutely nothing—about the genetic basis of love and virtue."[15]

A brief digression on cybernetics is appropriate here, since I am not dealing with it elsewhere in this book. By showing the similarities between the human brain and the electronic computer, cybernetics raises the same issues as microbiology. In some ways the issues are simplified, since the basic process is reduced to quantifiable electronic processes rather than to the far more intricate processes of molecular biology. By this time almost everybody knows that computers can do some things so much more quickly and efficiently than the human mind that people develop inferiority complexes thinking about the question. But it was Norbert Wiener, America's most famous specialist on cybernetics, who insisted that no reliance upon computers could spare man the privilege and burden of making moral decisions. So he urged, "Render unto man the things which are man's and unto the computer the things which are the computer's."[16] The choice of goals, moral decisions, and aesthetic appreciation, in Wiener's judgment, were human.

To be human is to be akin to the rest of nature, yet to enjoy and suffer those human qualities that are easier to recognize than to define: transcendence and freedom. "Moral rightness and wrongness," says Dobzhansky, "have meaning only in connection with persons who are free agents, and who are consequently able to choose between different ideas and between possible courses of action. Ethics presuppose freedom."[17]

As that living being in whom nature comes to self-consciousness, man obviously is not *entirely* free. He may never know exactly how far his freedom is continuous or discontinuous with some kind of spontaneity in the electron, the plant, and the animal. But he has learned in many a sad experience that to deny his freedom is to depreciate his humanity.

Chapter IX

A Debate Within Psychology

We can expect the dialogue with psychology to be illuminating to theology. Psychology provides information about man, about his behavior and motivation. It challenges, reinforces, or reinterprets many a theme in the Christian doctrine of man.

But we should not expect psychology to resolve the most controversial issues within the Christian doctrine of man. The reason is that psychology usually reruns the old debates within its own styles of thinking. On questions about the nature and good of man, the intradisciplinary controversies within psychology are as great as those within theology. On the big issues it is as futile to argue, "Psychology says thus and so," as to report, "Religion says thus and so." Psychology rivals the church in its tendency to sectarianism, and ecumenical movements within both groups meet the same problems.

In this chapter I am selecting for attention a single debate within contemporary psychology, a debate that has led to stimulating conversation between psychology and theology. I am omitting comment on those behavioristic psychologies that attempt to explain man in mechanistic terms, because the basic issues they raise are the same as those discussed in the preceding chapter on the biological sciences. Some psychologists give as completely deterministic an account of human behavior as any biologist or geneticist can give. It is a different account; the psychologists usually disagree with the biologists' accounts and the biologists think the psychologists' accounts are all wrong. But the basic issues are those we have already investigated.

Hence, this chapter looks at a quite different issue. It is raised by those psychologists who investigate the whole man—his biology and his thought, his reflexes and his aspirations, his drive to survive and his moral aspirations. It is the issue of moral struggle. Is man inherently involved in conflicts that require a struggle against destructive impulses? Or is he a being who will rather readily achieve health and maturity if released from cramping inhibitions and unhealthy social structures? This discussion parallels a traditional theological discussion about human nature and sin. The controversy emerges clearly in the contrast between Sigmund Freud, the pioneer psychoanalyst, and the later revisionists, who modify the sternness of Freud's doctrine.

Freud was, in a curious way, an heir and ally of the theological tradition. I say "in a curious way," because the antagonisms between Freud and the theological tradition are obvious. These must be noted, if only in passing.

The first point of conflict is Freud's attack upon belief in God as a projection of man's unconscious fears and wishes. Too often Christians have tried to refute Freud without noticing the ways in which he is an heir of the Scriptures. The Biblical prophets also attacked those idols which terrified people with imaginary threats or offered illusory security from real threats. Freud's attack on neu-

rotic religion is notably akin to the theological criticism
of religion that has become so common in our time—and
that owes something to Freud. (I shall come back to this
theme in Chapter XIV.) Even so, the Freudian criticism
is sharp enough to make an uncomfortable relation with
Christian faith.[1]

Freud creates a second conflict on the issue of human
freedom. On one side of his thought, he offers reductive
explanations of human behavior. The seemingly purpose-
ful act becomes the result of blind impulses or of mechanisms produced in the self by childhood experiences. This
is not the only side of Freud. Furthermore, Christian
thought has always had its own perplexities about the
relation between human freedom and the bondage of the
will. So it will not do to claim an absolute opposition here.
But, again, the issue is real.

A third conflict arises over Freud's paradoxical rationalism. The man who undermined so many illusions about
the power of reason, who showed that a seemingly powerful reason is often the slave of irrational instinct and impulse, maintained an ideal of rationalism. His interpretation of human behavior was a secularized version of
Augustine's doctrine of the primacy of the will, but his
hopes were for the primacy of the intellect. "The primacy
of the intellect certainly lies in the far, far, but still probably not infinite, distance."[2] Despite the penetrating imagination he often demonstrated, Freud's own doctrine of
rational truth was rather literal and unimaginative.

Christian thinking does not reject all of Freud's hopes
for reason. His idea of the "development of mankind"[3]
is not totally alien to the theological declaration that man
has "come of age." His analysis of religious myths has
some relation to the theological demythologizing that has

become common today. But the relation between Freud's rationalism and the Christian sense of mystery and grace involves a real clash.

Even in these conflicts, as we have just looked at them, Freud is not the total enemy of Christian insight. On some other issues his thinking has a powerful Biblical bent. Freud looked at man entire. He saw a striving, struggling person, whose proudest thoughts are inherently related to irrational impulses. He saw the relation between mental and biological processes. He rejected that long tradition, running from Plato's *Phaedo* through Descartes's *Meditations,* which separates the mind from the body.

Above all, Freud was morally serious, as Philip Rieff has shown convincingly in his book, *Freud: The Mind of the Moralist.*[4] Freud, it has often been observed, was a kind of secularized Puritan. He understood the conflicts between man's destructive, antisocial impulses and the needs of community. Man lives in a perpetual dilemma. He needs culture, depends upon it for survival and meaning; yet he resents and fights it. The ego becomes torn between the demands of the superego, incorporating the requirements of society, and the lawless cravings of the id. In this warfare, Freud concludes, "every individual is virtually an enemy of culture," and "every culture must be built up on coercion and instinctual renunciation."[5]

Freud suggests that we look at the Biblical commands to love our neighbors and to love our enemies, as if we were confronting them for the first time. We would respond with astonished questions: "Why should we do this? What good is it to us? Above all, how can we do such a thing? How could it possibly be done?"[6] The Christian, reading Freud, may here find himself closer to the excitement of the Bible than to the thousands of platitudinous vulgarizations of love that infiltrate the affluent society.

The consequence of Freud's conception of human nature was a recognition of the importance of moral struggle in the life of man. Granted, he judged that modern civilization was in some ways unnecessarily repressive and should be modified to permit some gratifications often not tolerated.[7] This is the side of Freud that has been exploited by popular Freudianism. But Freud himself believed that inner conflict remains part of the human situation. Psychoanalysis can free buried destructive desires from harmful repression, but cannot eliminate them. "The repression is supplanted by a condemnation carried through with the best means at one's disposal."[8] The best means may mean a sublimation that redirected inner energies, especially sexual. "To the contributions of the energy won in such a way for the functions of our mental life we probably owe the highest cultural consequences."[9]

Freud's own value system was a tragic-aesthetic humanism with an aim that he thought not entirely inconsistent with religious faith: "the brotherhood of man and the reduction of suffering."[10] And in the conflict between man's two "primal instincts," Eros and Death, his hope was that "eternal Eros" "will put forth his strength so as to maintain himself alongside of his equally immortal adversary."[11]

It is understandable that a culture in revolt against its Puritan heritage should rebel likewise against this Freudian understanding of man. Hence contemporary psychology has brought a series of revisions of Freudianism. Sometimes the revisionists are able to appeal to empirical evidence in a persuasive way. Thus some of what Freud attributed to instinct is now attributed to culture. The general opinion is that Freud tended to universalize into "human nature" the behavior patterns of the nineteenth-

and twentieth-century Viennese—and perhaps of a particular subculture among these.

With this greater attention to culture comes a softening of the hostility that Freud saw between man and society. The conflict is not so bitter, the fixed positions on both sides not so unyielding. Hence there may be less need than Freud saw for coercion and instinctual renunciation. Perhaps man can live in a nonrepressive harmony with culture.

Among the existentialist psychotherapists—a minority, but an impressive group—is a serious concern for human freedom. They seek to correct the reductionism and the tendency to mechanistic explanations sometimes apparent in Freud. They develop a conception of the self that distinguishes between neurotic anxiety and the anxiety that is inherent in selfhood. Their concern is for the human in man and the human relationships that help to define the self and society. Hence they assert the importance of freedom, decision, and love in the face of the dehumanizing forces of contemporary culture.

In the combination of these post-Freudian tendencies there sometimes emerge an idealism and a hopefulness that are quite congenial to the new humanism. As Seymour Rubenfeld puts it, psychoanalytic thought has become, at its best, "a champion of our humanistic traditions in an inhuman age."[12]

If Freud was in some respects a secularized Puritan, his psychological insights fitted in some ways the neo-orthodox theologies of the past generation. Some theologians, drawing their doctrines specifically from Biblical revelation, were not interested in the dialogue with psychology; but others found certain affinities with Freud. They could argue with him on many points, but they and he were tough-minded. He gave them something they could get their teeth into, and his description of the human condition offered grist for their doctrine of man and sin.

The revisionists similarly fit rather well the new theological humanism. Their concern for human values and for self-fulfillment, their attacks of externally imposed authority, their aspirations and social idealism, their criticisms of contemporary society—all go with the increasing esteem for man among the humanistic theologians.

The question is whether they have gone soft. Is their conception of man too gentle? Are they too indulgent toward man, too ready to remove guilt complexes and overlook the reality of guilt? Are they too utopian?

This is the accusation of Philip Rieff in his astringent book, *The Triumph of the Therapeutic*. Rieff sees Freud's tough scientific analysis of man and the difficulty of morality replaced by a more tolerant spirit that is gentle to man for the sake of therapy. Although his specific targets are chiefly three thinkers—Carl G. Jung, Wilhelm Reich, and D. H. Lawrence—his criticism reaches into the heart of modern culture as well as of psychotherapy. He sees our society rejecting Freud's ethic of the moral demand and of moral struggle, replacing it with a spirit of self-acceptance —that is, acceptance of the imperfect self as it is.

Satirizing the new style of confidence and complacency, Rieff says, "Evil and immorality are disappearing, as Spencer assumed they would, mainly because our culture is changing its definition of human perfection."[13] As for the common ideal of self-realization, he asks, "What would suit the therapeutic ideal better than the prevalent American piety toward the self?"[14]

We can see some of the issues by contrasting the psychology of morality in Freud and in our own contemporary, Erich Fromm. Where Freud sees the individual virtually at war with society, Fromm thinks that persons who understand "the art of loving"[15] can live in harmony with culture when man achieves "the sane society."[16] Will Herberg has drawn the contrast between the two:

Where Freud is dualistic, Fromm is harmonistic; where Freud is somber, even pessimistic, Fromm exhibits an amazing confidence in the possibilities of human progress; where Freud assumes the posture of a disillusioned observer, Fromm is always the reformer.[17]

For Freud the commandment to love the neighbor is astonishing: "Nothing is so completely at variance with original human nature as this."[18] But as Fromm sees it, man, if "given a chance," strives for a mental health which means that he "relates himself to the world lovingly," and "accepts willingly the rational authority of conscience and reason."[19]

Fromm, I should immediately add, does not think that love is easy. It is a "rare achievement," requiring "true humility, courage, faith and discipline."[20] But the reason for the difficulty does not lie in Freud's ineradicable instinct (which is somewhat akin to original sin in traditional theology). The difficulty is, in part, simply that of maturing—of outgrowing infant narcissism and fixation on mother and clan. It is in part due to the nature of a competitive, capitalistic, commodity-greedy society, which requires love to be a marginal phenomenon of the nonconformist.[21] In a society of "humanistic communitarianism"[22] man will learn to love neighbor and self in harmony.

We can place both these positions in relation to the classical Christian doctrine of man. Freud tends to view man as though the original datum were his fallen nature,

not his creation in the image of God—although occasionally in his description of an "eternal Eros" he suggests
something else. Fromm views man as though there were
no really fallen nature, except for a thoroughly fallen social system.

In writing a judgment like that, I do not mean to imply
that theology glibly answers the debate between Freud
and his revisers. For theology, like psychology, wrestles
continuously with the issue of man's nature—and specifically with the question of whether man wages a struggle
from which he can be rescued only by the healing grace
of forgiveness or whether his created vitalities themselves
can guide him to salvation.

The theological issue is stated directly in the New
Testament. "I came that they may have life, and have it
abundantly." (John 10:10.) That is the charter of a Christian humanism. "If any man would come after me, let
him deny himself and take up his cross and follow me."
(Matt. 16:24.) That describes the cost of the humanism.
Christian thought constantly seeks to understand the experience of the grace that is a free, yet costly gift.

In assessing contemporary culture, Rieff states the comparable issue in this contrast: "Religious man was born
to be saved; psychological man was born to be pleased."[23]
In the relation between these two propositions, the new
humanism must discover its own meaning.

At this point, psychology, an invaluable partner in the
dialogue, will not deliver the verdict. For psychology, as
much as theology, depends upon the assumptions and insights of the psychologist.

The man studied by psychology is an ethical being; and
psychology must study his ethical feelings, behavior, and
conflicts. The psychologist is himself an ethical being. If

he sets aside his ethic for the sake of scientific observation, he distorts himself and skews the data that he finds. If he lets his own ethical sensitivities influence his judgment, he works from faith no less than the theologian.

Hence we may expect continuing diversity among psychologists on the issues that matter most. They bring their unique observations to the dialogue, but they show the same diversity of judgment that we find in poets and prophets and theologians. Unanimity is not to be expected on the doctrine of man. Every man's judgment on this subject is in part his assessment of external evidence and in part his understanding of himself.

CHAPTER X

Issues from the Social Sciences

The social sciences have a double impact upon man's self-understanding. In the first place, they provide an immense body of information about man, information sometimes suspected, sometimes quite unknown before scientific methods confirmed or discovered it. In the second place, they change the actual organization of society, thereby influencing men's behavior and the self-images that develop out of behavior.

The social sciences are relatively young. Their growth and proliferation in the last generation has been spectacular. Because their subject is man in society, theology can engage them in dialogue at many points. This chapter will sample the dialogues at only two points, corresponding to the double impact I have just mentioned. The first example will concern an informational issue; the second, an issue of the recognizable effect upon life of the social sciences.

The first issue concerns cultural diversity and the unity of man. In some respects all men resemble each other; they are recognizably human, rather than canine, feline, reptilian, or avian. In other respects there are vast differences between the caveman and metropolitan man, between the Eskimo and the Pigmy.

Modern sociology—more particularly, cultural anthropology—has shown the great variety of human societies. It emphasizes that the individual is a product of his culture, which gives him language, social institutions, a style of life, education, habits, even emotional responses. There are many styles of social organization, of behavior, and of feelings in the many human cultures. Modern anthropology, to quote Steward and Shimkin, has shown "the variety and uniqueness of innumerable cultural configurations and sequences, the diversity and relativism of cultural goals and logics, and the functional coherence of cultures in their own frames of reference."[1] All this has been disturbing to people who tend to assume that there is only one normal way of life—their own. As John Dewey once put it, "At some place on the globe, at some time, every kind of practice seems to have been tolerated or even praised."[2]

Theology, by comparison, has always put considerable emphasis on the unity of man. It teaches a unity of mankind in creation, a unity in need and in sin, a unity in final destiny. (Sometimes the duality is more conspicuous than the unity in ultimate destiny.) This Christian universalism has in practice often been distorted, innocently or maliciously. A Western form of Christianity became normative for the understanding of man. Those versions of theology influenced by Aristotle, in particular, saw man as a being with a fixed nature, and the experience of man in the Orient or in inner Africa did not enter into the doctrine of man.

To contemporary anthropology such a doctrine appears naïve. Instead of a fixed human nature, anthropology sees diversity; instead of the natural law of ethics, a variety of mores; instead of eternal moral principles, infinite diversity of custom.

Protestant theology since Luther has been highly critical of Aristotelian models. And the renaissance of Biblical theology in the past generation has made historical dynamism a fundamental motif. Karl Barth wrote, "The man who is hankering after the so-called 'eternal verities' had best, if he is determined not to be converted, leave his faith uncontaminated with Christian faith."[3] The content of Christian revelation is "never to be conceived and reproduced by us as a general truth"; revelation is reconciling activity, the Word of God specifically addressed to a person and evoking a unique response in him.[4]

Even so, the conflict with cultural anthropology persists. Barth could say that the differences between the time of Paul and our time are, theologically speaking, "purely trivial." "If we rightly understand ourselves, our problems are the problems of Paul: and if we be enlightened by the brightness of his answers, those answers must be ours."[5] The anthropologist at the same time (1918) was more likely to point out the remoteness between Paul's cultural situation and our own.

During the high tide of neo-orthodoxy, there was little conversation between theology and cultural anthropology. Sometimes it seemed that the two disciplines had no common world of discourse. More recently conversation has opened up, made possible by some modification of stance on both sides of the dialogue.

Theology has become increasingly aware of religious and cultural pluralism, both on a global scale and within so complex a society as that of the United States. The obvious reason has been the sheer pressure of facts. But the facts have reminded theology of its own heritage. As philosopher Robin G. Collingwood told the theologians, in Christian thinking "peoples and nations considered collectively are not eternal substances but have been created by God. And what God has created He can modify by a reorientation of its nature towards fresh ends; thus by the operation of His grace He can bring about development in the character of a person or a people already created."[6] This style of Christian historical thinking makes possible conversation with the anthropologist's cultural thinking.

Meanwhile the social sciences, as Yinger has pointed out, have undergone some change from "the extreme relativism that characterized an earlier sociology."[7] Steward and Shimkin, the anthropologists whom I quoted a few paragraphs back, point to several discoveries of the 1930's and after: "recurrent similarities in the social structures of simple hunting and fishing peoples; . . . extensive parallelisms in the development of agriculturally based, urbanized states in the Old and New Worlds; and . . . independently replicated behavior, such as the rise of messianic cults, in response to similar types of sociopsychological stress."[8]

When conversations open up, it turns out that both theology and anthropology are concerned with a common problem. How is cultural diversity related to common human values, to a widely shared human situation, and to international, intercultural brotherhood? The questions have been raised in a fascinating way by Ruth Benedict in her influential *Patterns of Culture*. This book, probably more than any other, impressed a wide public with the realization that personality develops within cultural relations and institutions, that each culture has its own characteristics, and that human acts must be understood within their own cultures. This understanding has great importance for people, including Christians, who are too quick to impose their own cultural standards upon others. Christian moralists, for example, need to recognize that bare breasts on Bali are not analogous to topless bathing suits on the Riviera, that polygamy may be a faithful and responsible form of family life within some cultures, that American-style elections are not a necessity for participatory democracy in every situation.

But there is another side to Dr. Benedict's anthropology. Although she sometimes wrote as a fervent cultural relativist, she could also make sweeping moral judgments—and in this regard she represented the divided mind of anthropology. There is not the slightest doubt that she regarded some cultures as healthier than and morally superior to others. Crane Brinton has shrewdly observed that anthropologists—like Ruth Benedict and Margaret Mead—are playing a skillful game of offering advice to American culture through their studies of quite different cultures.[9]

Furthermore, Dr. Benedict found that some behavioral traits reappear virtually everywhere. One of these is prejudice. All societies, she wrote, insist upon "the difference in kind between 'my own' closed group and the outsider. All primitive tribes agree in recognizing this category of the outsiders, those who are not only outside the provisions of the moral code which holds within the limits of one's own people, but who are summarily denied a place anywhere in the human scheme."[10] Each society then claims to be a chosen people, to practice the authentic way of life, to represent the truly human culture which must not be lost or corrupted by outsiders. "We are not likely to clear ourselves easily of so fundamental a human trait, but we can at least learn to recognize its history and its hydra manifestations."[11] It is easy to recognize in such a description the likeness to the theological doctrine of sin.

In her anthropological investigations of religion, Dr.

Benedict came to similar conclusions. With most observers she first saw the tremendous diversity among men in beliefs and practices. But she went on to observe: "The striking fact about this plain distinction between the religious and the nonreligious in actual ethnographic recording is that it needs so little recasting in its transfer from one society to another."[12]

Will Herberg has pointed out that the contemporary scientific mind lives in an "uneasy hesitation between a sociological relativism and the effort to find some fixed point in a 'pan-human' normative type."[13] The data support his judgment. He might have added that theology lives in a similar uneasiness. Its dialogue with sociology and anthropology have helped it cleanse itself of many a provincialism and dogmatism. Now it seeks to interrogate once again its own traditions and its own culturally conditioned formulations in order to discover what of its tradition it must revise, what it shall decide to retain as a valued particular heritage within a pluralistic mankind, and what it should declare to the world as of divine-human import. In these decisions the continuing dialogue with the social sciences will play a major part.

The second issue I have chosen for attention in this chapter concerns not so much knowledge about man as control of man. The social sciences discover the structures and processes that determine many aspects of the life of man in society. Such knowledge is power. It can be applied to reshape society. It changes the conditions of life and man's understanding of himself.

The most familiar example comes from economics. Modern economists have discovered many of the mechanisms that operate in the economic cycle. The "new economics," stemming from John Maynard Keynes, provides the methods for stimulating or damping production and consumption. Thus it moderates the processes that formerly led to booms and crashes. Today, despite all the controversies about economic policies, there is general agreement that government is remiss if it permits either runaway inflation or a high percentage of unemployment. Although the instruments of economic measurement and control are not so precise as those of a physics laboratory, they work.

Such an achievement may seem to be, in principle, an unqualified gain. It transfers an area of human life from fate to intelligent decision. It prevents formerly inevitable catastrophes and increases the security of families. Nevertheless, men sometimes fear and distrust the new power of control. The reason is that economics always involves conflicts of power. The person or group who controls the mechanisms inevitably gains power over the society and the people in it.

Such fears swiftly escalate as the controls impinge increasingly on personal life. Men do not want to be manipulated by experts, even when the experts promise that the manipulation is for the public good.

Some social scientists insist that their discipline is a rigorous science, free from value judgments and ambitions to change the world. But the social sciences *are* changing the world, and everybody recognizes that they are. Sociology, the most comprehensive of the social sciences, has had a divided mind about its own function, starting with its founder, August Comte (1798–1857). Comte was, on the one hand, a "positivist," trying to establish a social physics. He wanted to leave behind the theological and metaphysical ages of history and inaugurate the positive age, when men would explain phenomena through observation, hypothesis, and verification. He was, on the other hand, a crusader seeking to reform society and establish a new religion of humanity.

Comte's successors have followed both of his impulses. Some have exploited his positivism. Wanting to make sociology more like physics, they emphasize quantifiable data and seek to avoid value judgments. Others retain something of Comte's messianism. Albert Salomon in *The Tyranny of Progress,* a study of the history of French sociology, shows how the devotion to an ideal society led Comte's heirs to totalitarian theories, by which an elite should manipulate and control society for the sake of progress.[14]

Whether or not the social scientist himself is ambitious to shape the course of society, he provides the understanding by which policy makers in power can do so. One distinguished sociologist, Howard Becker, has argued that science can eliminate all value judgments except *"the supreme value judgment that control is ultimately desirable".*[15]

The scientist becomes a priest of the faith in the possibility and supreme desirability of control. The secular society in which he has grown up and which sanctions his preference-system is endowed with sacred values by his enterprise; the quest for control becomes a quest for the Holy Grail. Nonrational? Yes! What ultimate values have ever been rational? Impartial? No! What priest was ever impartial?[16]

By control, Becker means at a minimum the hypothetical control that is part of the scientific method. He recognizes that such control readily leads to the actual, practical control of social processes, and because of the dangers of such control, he argues for "value-polytheism."

Here we come back to the issue I touched on in Chapter VI. In a technological society the good of everybody is involved in the good of everybody else—whether the issue be war, full employment, urban transportation, air pollution, or crime in the ghettos. Society inevitably adopts greater controls, and the judgment of experts becomes increasingly necessary to make the controls work. Who but the expert can possibly devise a system of inspection of armaments, or set the specifications for reducing exhaust fumes from automobiles, or design adequate urban housing? Popular opinion is helpless on these issues, unless informed by experts.

But men and women at large have two justifiable fears of the expert. They wonder whether the experts are using their power for the public good or for the sake of themselves—since experts, like the rest of us, have their human prejudices and advantages. And they wonder whether the experts are manipulating the public to the point that—even with the best of motives—they are turning people into things.

Social psychologist Donald N. Michael has made a brilliant analysis of the promise and threat of the immediate future on just this issue. "During the next two decades," he wrote in 1963, "belief in man as unique in himself and in his relation to the rest of the universe will, in many of the influential decision-making and policy-planning levels of society, become substantially secondary to viewing him as subject to the same manipulation and attention as other dynamic parts of social and physical systems."[17]

The causes of this tendency will be medical technology (see Chapter VIII), "social engineering," and the whole process of "rationalization" of society (in the sense of the application of means to achieve desired ends). Probably there is not one of these processes that men will want to stop, although they may worry about them all.

Michael expects protests. "There will also be an increasingly vocal body of informed opinion asserting that man is infinitely more than a manipulable thing and that, indeed, our troubles stem from treating him as if that were all he is."[18] The answer to such trepidations may be only a "ritual acknowledgment" of man's uniqueness, of the kind already found in policy documents. But something more may emerge. "Over the long run, as unhappy experience leads to understanding that rationalization involves more than logic and computer-encompassable efficiency, this humanistic viewpoint may begin to carry real weight."[19]

One possible conclusion is that the issue of whether man is a manipulable object will depend upon what he decides or allows himself to become. His self-understanding will influence his decisions; and his decisions will influence his self-understanding.

CHAPTER XI

The Affair with Existentialism

For more than a century a love-hate affair has been going on between theology and existentialism. The affair was inevitable. Existentialism erupted within theology, with Søren Kierkegaard as its creative protagonist. It has lived out its stormy career in mixed dependence upon and defiance of its Christian sources. Theology, not able to discipline its unruly offspring, has both cherished and resented existentialism.

By existentialism I mean both a philosophy and a cultural movement. When theology seeks dialogue with philosophy, it promptly meets existentialism, which of all contemporary philosophies is most immediately concerned with man. When theology enters into dialogue with culture, it again meets existentialism in the arts and in the style of behavior of many men.

Existentialism is alive and chaotic. Its pioneers and elder statesmen include the diverse array of Kierkegaard, Dostoevsky, Nietzsche, Heidegger, Jaspers, Buber, Bultmann, and Sartre. Obviously it is not a philosophy of consensus. Hence, Christian theology, which has its own freedom and inner variety, cannot take any one clear attitude toward existentialism. Today most Christian thinking about man is thoroughly existentialist—at the very least in the sense that it considers man in his actual existence, not in abstraction. But theology also shows signs of weariness with or rejection of existentialism. To understand this ambivalent attitude, it is necessary to look at two prominent themes within existentialism.

The first of these is the theme of personal freedom. One of the deepest impulses in existentialism is the assertion of selfhood, the yearning to rescue man from dehumanization, the insistence upon the assertion of persons in free decisions. Paul Tillich describes the origins of nineteenth-century existentialism as follows:

It was the threat of an infinite loss, namely the loss of their individual persons, which drove the revolutionary Existentialists of the 19th century to their attack. They realized that a process was going on in which people were transformed into things, into pieces of reality which pure science can calculate and technical science can control.[1]

Existentialists, although they lack any passion for unanimity, can unite in a cry of protest against whatever stifles man and his freedom. Their protest is, sometimes hiddenly and sometimes openly, an affirmation. In one way or another they celebrate the wonder—the delight and the terror—of being human. They call man not to submerge himself in the impersonal processes of modern history, but to assert his authentic existence. They beckon man to come out of the anonymous, conformist herd and exercise his own freedom in responsible decision.

In its many styles, existentialism may be devout or blasphemous, crude or subtle, individualistic or interpersonal. It recognizes and quarrels over many virtues. But it concurs in lifting up the major virtue of freedom, of courage, of decision, of the assertion of man against all the forces that try to stifle him.

Existentialism identifies the enemy in many ways. Sometimes the enemy is technology, turning the social organism into a machine, subjecting persons to processes, mechanizing life and human relations. Sometimes it is the organization, fitting people into impersonal slots for the sake of efficiency. Sometimes it is the utilitarian morality that takes the anguish and turmoil out of decision by turning ethics into a calculating science of the means toward the self-evident end of happiness. Sometimes it is external authority, imposing itself upon man and denying him the dignity of being himself. Sometimes it is the mass communications that saturate man in the ideology of the affluent society. Sometimes it is the very concept of objectivity, which stands over against the subjective and personal, claiming validity entirely apart from the human involvement that would undermine or transform it.

In all these cases the enemy is anything that destroys the personal. Human life, says the existentialist, is personal existence, involvement, commitment, decision, the risk of being oneself. Values are human and have no meaning apart from human concern. In short, "Existentialism is a Humanism," to use the title of Jean-Paul Sartre's most famous essay.

Clearly, then, Christian thought about man must take account of existentialism. There are many disputes among Christians, among existentialists, and among Christian existentialists about the relation of individuality to community and of freedom to authority. But the new theological humanism has nourished itself on existentialism.

Yet there is an increasing estrangement between Christian humanism and existentialism. To the new humanist existentialism may appear as a part of the romantic movement, unwilling to enter the contemporary world, unable to participate in the revolutionary history of modern man. It may seem to belong to the aesthetes rather than the doers, to the alienated rather than the activists.

Dietrich Bonhoeffer, in seeking a "religionless Christianity," directed one of his major thrusts against what he called inwardness or individualism.[2] In one way, this is surprising in Bonhoeffer. His prison poem, "Who Am I?"[3] is a powerful example of introspection, pushing below appearances to the inward realities of his own life. It belongs among the primary sources of existentialist theology. Its second stanza has a Kierkegaardian anguish—even a Kierkegaardian vocabulary.

But Bonhoeffer's polemic comes clear in his refusal to confine God to an inward life:

When God was driven out of the world, and from the public side of human life, an attempt was made to retain him at least in the sphere of the "personal," the "inner life," the private life. . . . It is thought that man's essential nature consists of his inmost and most intimate background, and that is defined as his "interior life"; and it is in these secret human places that God is now to have his domain![4]

Against all such tendencies, Bonhoeffer insists that God is concerned with the whole man, with his full life rather than some inward fragment of it, with his strength as well as his weakness. He specifically objects to the use of existentialism and psychotherapy as "spiritual subterfuges" designed to drive man inward upon himself and soften him up for God.[5]

More recently Harvey Cox has taken up this theme. Cox has a divided mind on existentialism. He writes an occasional sentence that comes directly out of existentialism (Nietzsche via Sartre). "He [man] doesn't simply discover meaning; he originates it."[6] But often he scorns existentialism:

Existentialism . . . is the last child of a cultural epoch, born in its mother's senility. That is why existentialist writers seem so arcadian and antiurban. They represent an epoch marked for extinction. Consequently their thinking tends to be anti-technological, individualistic, romantic, and deeply suspicious of cities and of science.[7]

That language describes a specific and peculiar form of existentialism, but a recognizable form. It is probably fair to say of Cox that he joins existentialism in its affirmation of freedom but rejects its frequent introversion. There is in existentialism—or in some of its many varieties—a tendency to savor the inward experience in a rather precious way, to cultivate anxiety, to lure people to pretend to have authentic experiences that they are not always sure they really have.

One of the paradoxes of contemporary culture is that art has concentrated on the probing of the inward man in an epoch when history has recorded unusual exploits of man both in his social existence and in the mastery of his external environment. Nathan Scott has commented on the retreat of American fiction, for the most part, from "embattled social humanism" to privacy. Scott notes "a profound lack of faith in the possibility of the great, gross reality of society ever becoming anything with which the self might do any kind of significant business."[8]

Similarly the novelist John Updike has written a comment on J. D. Salinger, which might apply to the writings of Updike himself:

Introversion, perhaps, has been forced upon history; an age of nuance, of ambiguous gestures and psychological jockeying on a national and private scale, is upon us. . . . As Hemingway sought the words for things in motion, Salinger seeks the words for things transmuted into human subjectivity.[9]

But obviously this is a world where men do act, day in and day out, making decisions with momentous public consequences. The man of action often has no use for the involuted manner of the artist. Out of Washington has come a comment from a man described as a sub-Cabinet officer:

> My wife shoves these novels under my nose. I try to read them, and give up. Why should I spend my time on them? Without exception, those I have sampled turn out to be another case where the central character spends 350 pages quivering about whether to cross the street or go to the toilet. Every day, people like myself in the government face human problems that are far more interesting, complex and important than any yet dreamed about by the writers of the "serious" novels. What's more, it's our job to do something about those problems, not just to describe them, much less to quiver about them. I might feel differently if I didn't hold my present job. As it is, the "serious" novels which are supposed, as the reviewers say, "to illuminate the human condition" amount to egocentric blathering.[10]

In the light of that comment from a politician, it is understandable that some theologians are turning from the existentialist to the political sphere for theological vocabulary and concepts. The theologian learns as much about man from the political arena as from introspection. And the new humanism is at least as much concerned with civil rights, war in Vietnam, and the struggle against poverty as it is with the inner world of the existentialists.

Yet any valid humanism must concern itself with man's whole experience. If retreat to the inner world can be an evasion of social responsibility, it is equally true that activism can be an evasion of the hidden alienation and guilt of the self. Eric Hoffer has observed, "Mass movements are often the means by which a population undergoing drastic change acquires a sense of rebirth and a new identity."[11] The question for the individual, then, is whether the mass movement focuses or suppresses his identity and the issues of his personal life.

The French theologian, André Dumas, has said:

The Christian community would be at least one generation too late if it insisted only upon the political dimension of the Christian message which had been misunderstood by individ- ialistic pietism, now that the most important thing in our new society is that above all work and politics must not go too far afield and neglect the deeper side of personal life, love, holidays, culture and pleasure, which provide relaxation apart from the pressures of job and city life.[12]

Herbert Marcuse makes this fascinating observation: "The real face of our time shows in Samuel Beckett's novels; its real history is written in Rolf Hochhut's play *Der Stellvertreter*."[13] Beckett is the existentialist, ferreting out the inner conflicts of lonely man; Hochhut dramatizes the struggle of conscience in the titanic political act of the Nazi persecution of the Jews. What Marcuse—scholar of politics, psychology, and philosophy—sees is the intimate relation between the existentialist and the political themes. To neglect the political life (in at least the broad sense of that term) is to truncate one's humanity; but political man, like economic man and any other man who silences his inmost self, may be "one-dimensional man."

The new humanism at its best makes the heroic effort to humanize the political and economic world, while still appreciating those aspects of human life that are never totally comprehended in public institutions. To maintain an integral life in this fractured era of history is not easy. This is the day of the two cultures described by C. P. Snow in his famous book *The Two Cultures and the Scientific Revolution*.[14] Critics by this time have worked over Snow's thesis, modifying it or adding to his two cul- tures a third or fourth or indefinite number. But Snow surely points to a real cleft between those who exult in the scientific revolution and those who fear or disdain it, those who immerse themselves in public life and those who feel the tremors of the individual, the often insensitive operators and the highly sensitive rebels. The dichotomy is not only between two groups of people; it divides many a person.

Yale psychologist Kenneth Keniston has made one of the most perceptive reports on the college campus in this era when almost everybody is diagnosing the student generation. Keniston reports that the "Big Man on Campus" is fading. The leader of the early twentieth century, the man who cultivated popularity and social skills, the youth oriented to his peer group and at home in the student culture, is on the way out. In his place "the new campus hero is becoming the committed *professionalist* who is 'really good in his field.' "[15] He cultivates the "technological virtues" and values "technical, intellectual, and professional competence above popularity, ambition, or grace."[16] All this does not mean that he is highly intellectual. Rather, "his public goals are only to do better the same kind of thing that his father did"—in the same "professional, suburban" style of life.[17]

The trouble is that this professionalist finds little personal meaning in his professionalism. Hence, "the gap between public persona and private self is very great." The result is an intense privatism in the search for meaning and identity:

The vehicle of this search is inevitably personal and expressive: friendship, music, art, sports, dramatics, or even poetry. . . . The most casual friendship may involve a painful search for self-definition; and reading, walking in the country, or listening to music can become part of the "quest for identity."[18]

The new humanism has an immense task on its hands, both in its effort to formulate a doctrine of man that takes account of his whole nature and in its effort to contribute to the integrity of man in the contemporary church and world. Faith cannot humanize life unless it finds relevance to the rival cultures that divide modern society and so many persons. In the effort, the conversation with existentialism, the champion of man's freedom and the discloser of his despair, will play a continuing part.

Chapter XII

Renewed Conversations with Marxism

The new humanism has revived the old Christian-Marxist dialogue. This dialogue has a long history. Christian-Communist relations from the beginning showed a combination of affinity and hostility, as remarkable as the love-hate affair we have just noted between Christianity and existentialism.

There was an ethical impulse in Marx that owed much to the Biblical tradition. He sometimes felt embarrassment over this dependence and made angry efforts to show that he was not Christian. But his famous slogan, "From each according to his abilities, to each according to his need" (1875), had a long Christian history. It expressed the practice of the Christians in New Testament times (Acts 4:32–37) and of monastic communities through the centuries. New England Puritans used it in the seventeenth century,[1] and Louis Blanc's *Socialist Catechism* of 1849 sloganized it in a Christian context three decades ahead of Marx.

Furthermore, as a wide range of scholars has pointed out, the Marxist interpretation of history is a secularization of the Christian dramatic representation of history. Marxism has its creation in innocence, its fall, its history of estranged man, its messianic people (the proletariat), messianic age, millennium, and final Kingdom of God— all in thoroughly secularized forms.[2]

Hence, Marx has always attracted some Christians, as he has repelled others. Following World War II and the Soviet revolution, Christian thought gave considerable attention to Marxism. In Great Britain, John Macmurray, leader of "the Christian Left," worked toward "a synthesis" of Christianity and Communism. In Germany the very different "religious socialism" of Paul Tillich and Eduard Heimann showed critical appreciation of Marxism. In the United States the left wing of the social gospel appropriated Marxist themes, sometimes romantically and sometimes cautiously. I have already noted (Chapter IV) the way in which the Marxist analysis of power influenced Reinhold Niebuhr's doctrine of man.

But despite these many evidences of Christian interest in Marxism, the dialogue always ran into trouble. On the one side, the dominant conservatism of the churches resisted, sometimes with angry dogmatism, anything Marxist. On the other side, Marxism showed deep hostility— possibly an Oedipal hostility—to anything Christian, as evidenced by Marx's denunciations of religious socialism in his own time.

Furthermore, the best-intentioned Christian efforts at dialogue ran into the horrors of Stalinism. The relation of Stalinism to Marxism is still much debated. Today the humanistic Marxist would like to say that Stalin is no more related to Marx than Torquemada to Jesus, but during the Stalinist era nobody said that. Some still suspect that the combination of utopian goals with ruthless methods in Marxism led rather easily through Leninism to Stalinism.

Not even Stalinism could entirely stop conversations between Christians and Communists as persons. During the most bitter period of the cold war, some personal communication continued. When Americans thought of Communists, in those days, they usually thought immediately of ideology and military power. Europeans were more likely to think first of their neighbors, who were people. Christians could meet Communists as persons, without always rushing immediately into the ideological clash. Communists, even when they were exercising political authority, might be recognized as persons. They too got sick, had family problems, sometimes enjoyed a joke, or showed compassion. So conversations, arising out of common humanity, persisted between Christians and Marxists, even when conversation between Christianity and Marxism was suspended.

With the end of Stalinism new possibilities for dialogue appeared. Communism had never been quite the international monolithic system that both Stalinists and conventional anti-Communists had tried to make it. A few years after Stalin anybody not blinded by ideological fury could see immense variety within Communism. The third of the world that is more or less Marxist includes great contrasts in social organization, economic practices, technological development, cultural styles, and relations with other parts of the world. To ignore or oppose everything in this world is nonsensical. In an age when technology has produced monstrous destructive powers, the safety of the world demands at least a willingness for conversation. Humanism goes farther: it craves conversation.

Furthermore, Marx himself provides the opening for conversation. On one side of this thought Marx was a passionate humanist. His description of man's alienation and the possibility of reconciliation has an instant familiarity to anyone in the Christian tradition. This theme is developed in Marx's early *Economic and Philosophical Manuscripts* (1844). As Daniel Bell has shown, the idea was not original with Marx, and Marx himself did not consider it his important contribution.[3] The orthodox Marxist development through Lenin and Stalin was uninterested in it. But its rediscovery at a time when the idea of alienation has hypnotic fascination for a worried mankind affords a powerful stimulus to Christian-Marxist conversations.

For many years Paul Tillich was the only eminent American philosopher or theologian to give major attention to Marx's treatment of alienation. The basic Marxist documents remained untranslated and little read. But then their English translation made a sizable splash. When edited and interpreted by Erich Fromm,[4] they produced a picture of a young Marx, who was a humanist remarkably like Fromm.

This humanistic Marx described alienation in its many facets. Man is alienated from the product of his labor, from his own activity (which is to say, from himself), from his species-being (a phrase from Feuerbach that is almost a secular equivalent of the image of God), from other men, from nature. Science is alienated from morality. In one summary, Marx holds that the existing industrial system "alienates from man his own body, external nature, his mental life and his *human* life."[5] Thus *"an inhuman power* rules over everything."[6] Against this power Marx seeks "the emancipation of humanity as a whole."[7] He looks for "a new emancipation of *human* powers and a new enrichment of the human being."[8]

Clearly such ideas are grist for the new humanism. They

open rich possibilities for Christian-Marxist conversation. Such conversations might run into a swift block if Marxists should insist (with Marx in most but not all of his moods) that the sole cause and cure of alienation is the economic and class structure. But Marxists these days are not making that insistence. So when Christians are able to relax their dogmatic opposition to Marxism, they find openings for genuine dialogue with dedogmatized Marxists.

One phase of the dialogue has developed in Western Europe, especially France, and has reached into North America. It won wide public attention when the Roman Catholic publisher, Herder & Herder, Inc., brought out two books in 1966 as its contribution to the dialogue: from the French Marxist, Roger Garaudy, *From Anathema to Dialogue: A Marxist Challenge to the Christian Churches;* and from the Canadian Catholic, Leslie Dewart, *The Future of Belief: Theism in a World Come of Age.* At the time of publication Garaudy visited the United States for a series of lectures and discussions. A society accustomed to the traditional Catholic rejection of "atheistic Communism" was surprised to find Catholics introducing to America this philosopher, who is not only a Marxist but also a member of the Central Committee of the French Communist Party.[9]

The attraction of Garaudy is that he wants true dialogue —not polemics, not compromise, not proselytizing, but dialogue. He enters the dialogue ready to learn as well as to persuade. Any Christian participating in the dialogue is likely to find real illumination on the nature of man.

Marxist hermeneutics turn out to be as complex as Christian hermeneutics. Both Marxists and Christians read their scriptures selectively, and both sometimes find surprises in their return to the sources.

Garaudy finds the humanistic and idealistic Marx, whom I have described above, rather than the ruthless polemicist who discards all moral inhibitions in his attack against class enemies. He finds the celebrant of freedom rather than the determinist analyzing the objective science of history. In this selection I think that Garaudy picks the most attractive choice and the choice that offers the most possibilities for dialogue.

Similarly, Garaudy selects from many possibilities the Christianity that he thinks can enter into the dialogue. It is not that Christianity which has been an instrument of oppression and an "opium of the people." Nor is it the Christianity of simple social idealism. It is that Christianity which discovered man as a free being, capable of risk and decision, destined to explore his own subjectivity, able to enter into a new future undictated by his past. It is the Christianity that discovered *agapē* in contrast to the classical *erōs*.

The fascination of Garaudy's invitation to dialogue is that he appreciates not only the Biblical ethic, with its concern for the poor and oppressed, but also the Biblical theology, with its sense of man, society, and history. He frankly disagrees with the Christian belief in God, but he thinks that Christian faith can make a genuine contribution to the understanding of man. Interestingly, in a period when some Christians, reading or misreading Dietrich Bonhoeffer's rejection of "inwardness," want to "go political," Garaudy values the Christian exploration of "interiority"—provided, of course, it is not made the means of escape from the urgent problems of society.

Christians, if they are willing to learn from this dialogue, will find a burning criticism of their own unconcern for mankind and their frequent readiness to let religion become an ideology for the comfortable and an opiate for the oppressed. They will find a reminder that Christian love can be misused as a pretext for ignoring the demands of justice, that Christian humility can be misused as a device of the powerful to label as immoral the protests of the weak. If it is said that Christians might learn all this from their own heritage, it must also be said that Christian institutions have frequently suppressed just such warnings, thus making necessary protests from outside the faith.

Christians can also learn from certain more specifically Marxist ideas. They can find an appreciation—perhaps exaggerated but real[10]—of the economic aspect of life. They can find an awareness of the functioning of ideology —of the ways in which men see the world in terms of their own positions of privilege or need. They may gain an awareness that the Christian sense of human relations, which the New Testament puts primarily in terms of the intimate community, must be extended to the institutions of an industrial society which enhance or destroy human freedom.

Christians can meet in the dialogue a specific criticism of the contemporary world, often abrasive, because that is the only kind of criticism which can get through. Roger Mehl, the French Christian philosopher, says:

And thanks to the presence of this man [Marxist man] in a world singularly drab and blasé, the terms "heroism," "courage," "abnegation," and "force" retain meaning and pungency. I do not believe that our Western civilization could have succeeded by itself in preserving the meaning of these words, preferring as it does the words "comfort," "well-being," "security."[11]

The dialogue needs to continue. I expect it to produce increasingly sharp and rich understanding. I expect also that it will run into difficulties. In its innocent eagerness, it is sometimes a little too confident and cheerful.

For example, Garaudy, in his generous and often perceptive interpretation of Christianity, has made this faith more pleasant than it really is. For example, he quotes with approval from Teilhard de Chardin a curious statement "that the universe is still progressing, and that we are in charge of this progress."[12] A Biblical prophet or a modern astronomer can quickly remind us that "we are in charge of" a pretty small bit of the universe and that (as Einstein used to observe) we have more trouble taking charge of ourselves than of our physical surroundings.

Although Garaudy reads the Christian sources with intelligence and imagination, he reads them through the Enlightenment and the romantic movement. Hence, his Faustian version of Christianity is strangely contradictory to the New Testament. He appropriates from Biblical eschatology its sense of the dynamism of history and of a future that gives meaning to the present, but he does not know what to do with its sense of divine grace.

The problem appears in the contrast that Garaudy draws between two styles of Christianity: the primitive, apocalyptic faith, with its accent on human initiative and its protest against the established order; and Constantinian Christianity, with its accent on sin and its justification of the ruling classes.[13] But there are problems of historical accuracy in this contrast. Where in primitive Christianity was apocalyptic faith detached from the accent on sin and forgiveness? Surely not in the New Testament. Garaudy, aiming to be kind to original Christianity, has removed too much of the offense that inherently belongs to it.

In Eastern Europe, the Christian-Marxist dialogue on the public level is somewhat inhibited by the officially

Marxist domination of the state. The literature of the East European languages is less accessible to us in the West, but we have many evidences, some public and some private, of significant dialogue there.[14] The inheritance of Dostoevsky—with his awareness of human anxiety and guilt, and his criticism of all official utopias, whether bourgeois or socialist—sometimes gives the Eastern dialogues a peculiar profundity.

Officially the Marxists must oppose Christian faith, regard it as an anachronism, champion secularization and militant humanism. Articles in the Eastern European press occasionally express perplexity at the persistence of religious faith and dissatisfaction with the propaganda against it. Only rarely do they give the grudging impression that the Christians—to use the phraseology of American advertising—"must be doing something right."

More often Marxist spokesmen open the way to dialogue, not by their comments about religion or God but by their analysis of the old Marxist theme of alienation. Increasingly they are ready to acknowledge that there is something about alienation that is not overcome by revolution and a new economic order. Helmut Gollwitzer, a Berlin theologian whose reputation certainly is not that of a dogmatic anti-Communist, reports: "A philosophical debate on alienation under communism is taking place inside some of the eastern European countries. Is man, after all, a more complicated phenomenon than orthodox communist philosophy allows for?"[15]

Much of the discussion goes on among writers and artists, who in Communist lands as elsewhere, chafe at the official philosophy of political leaders and bureaucrats. The controversies that have raged about Pasternak, Yevtushenko, Tvardovsky, and the journal *Novy Mir* are the most obvious evidence. Sergei P. Pavlov, first secretary of the Young Communist League, has protested publicly about a literature that is rather like the Western literature of interiorization. His complaint is that "some books and magazines, plays and movies are imbued with a note of unhealthy criticism, confined outlook on life, concern with petty events, glorification of suffering, preaching of hopelessness."[16] Its influence, he says, contributes to a mood of nihilism and indifference among youth—another comment that sounds familiar to Western ears.

Further evidence is not sufficient to provide massive documentation for Gollwitzer's statement, but there are many straws in the wind. For example, Adam Schaff, the Polish Communist, has stirred controversies by arguing that socialism "by no means signifies the end of alienation."[17] Gajo Petrovic, the Yugoslav Marxist, although he favors the socialization of property, says that such measures are not sufficient for overcoming alienation.[18] Milan Machovec, a Czech Marxist philosopher, in a book called *The Sense of Human Life,* sees much of the destiny of man in "inner dialogue" between persons.[19]

These comments and others like them are not part of a deliberate effort to enter into dialogue with Christians. That, for the most part, is still not approved in Eastern Europe. In fact, Communist writers frequently deny the validity of such dialogue, unless for the sole purpose of exposing the errors of religion. But the sensitivity to human problems provides the opportunity for conversation —if Christians do not seize upon them for propagandistic purposes.

The Christian response—a good example is in the writings and discussions of Josef L. Hromádka and J. M. Lochman, both of Prague—is to endorse much of the

Marxist drive toward secularization and humanism. The basis for the endorsement is not the Communist ideology but a Christology that owes much to Barth and Bonhoeffer. On this ground such Christians affirm their eagerness to cooperate with Communists toward all truly humanistic goals, their desire to abandon any ancient privileges of the church, and their fervent wish to live in a post-Constantinian age.

But they keep an awareness of the questions about man that social reform cannot answer. They find opportunity for dialogue when Marxists themselves raise questions of the nature of man, explore the experiences of alienation and reconciliation, inquire into human tragic experiences and potentialities. The resulting dialogue is not spectacular; but it is open, and no one can yet foresee where it may lead.

On rare occasions the dialogue becomes public. Thus Czech Communists, on the 550th anniversary of the martyrdom of John Hus, invited Catholic and Protestant scholars from the West to an international symposium on Hus (Aug. 18–21, 1965). A far more specific effort at dialogue took place in April of 1967 at Marienbad, Czechoslovakia, under the cosponsorship of the Paulus Society of Western Germany (an organization of theologians and scientists) and the Czech Academy of Sciences.[20] Among the participants were Roger Garaudy, Milan Machovec, and Erich Kellner of the Paulus Society. In general the attitudes were candid and irenic.

But an unsettling note was raised by Mauricio Lopez of Argentina, Secretary of the Department on Church and Society of the World Council of Churches. Lopez pointed out that the Christian-Marxist dialogue was taking place between persons from the wealthy societies and that the poor had been left out.

It would be one of the strangest and most tragic of historical ironies if Christians and Marxists should begin to find success in understanding each other at the cost of forgetting the concern for the poor that is so prominent in both traditions. At a few places in the world, most notably in impoverished lands of South America, a Christian-Marxist dialogue among the poor is under way, not conspicuously but searchingly. Obviously the more public dialogue must continue, but its scope must expand. We cannot expect the present generation to discover the last word about man; but the last word, even for our time, must remain hidden except as all men are heard.

PART THREE

New Shapes of Old Controversies

CHAPTER XIII

Does Man Have a Nature?

The new humanism is in many respects a polemical answer to nonhumanistic or antihumanistic positions. It takes sides. It intends to resolve issues—at least some issues —rather than analyze them endlessly.

But in other respects the new humanism is open. As we have seen, it welcomes dialogues with many disciplines and ideologies. It is an inquiry as much as a declaration.

Furthermore, within its ethos many an old issue, seemingly settled by the very advocacy of humanism, rises again. The final section of this book looks into five continuing controversies within current Christian thinking about the nature of man.

The first of these controversies, the subject of this chapter, centers in the old question: Does man have a nature? Does it make sense to talk about human nature? Artemus Ward used to say that everybody has as much human nature as everybody else, if not more. But what does it mean to speak of human nature?

The debate took its classical formulation in the Renaissance protest against scholasticism. The medieval doctrine of man, a combination of Aristotle's philosophy and one form of Biblical interpretation, located man in the fixed hierarchy of being—above the vegetables and animals, below the angels and archangels. It described man as created in the image of God, but the victim of the Fall. Henceforth, human possibilities are pretty definitely fixed. Redemption is available for a few, but the human social structures and the earthly potentialities of man are rather permanently settled by the requirements of nature and of sin. The popular version of this theology is the perennial cry, in answer to every proposal for social reform, "You can't change human nature." I should note in passing that, despite some Biblical elements in this doctrine, it is a highly abstract account of man compared with the concrete records of men and their actions in Scripture.

The Renaissance, exulting in the possibilities of man, rejected this scholastic doctrine. Pico della Mirandola in his *Oration on the Dignity of Man* proclaimed that the divine gift to man was not a fixed nature, like that of other species, but the freedom in which man could make of himself what he chose to be. Pico represented God as addressing man:

We have given to thee, Adam, no fixed seat, no form of thy very own, no gift peculiarly thine, that thou mayest feel as thine own, have as thine own, possess as thine own the seat, the form, the gifts which thou thyself shalt desire. A limited nature in other creatures is confined within the laws written down by Us. In conformity with thy free judgment, in whose hands I have placed thee, thou art confined by no bounds; and thou wilt fix limits of nature for thyself. . . . Thou, like a judge appointed for being honorable, art the molder and maker of thyself; thou mayest sculpt thyself into whatever shape thou dost prefer.[1]

The new humanism emphasizes the possibilities before man. It insists that many of the seemingly fixed patterns of human nature are actually cultural characteristics that can be changed. I have earlier (p. 98) quoted John Dewey's statement about the great diversity of human behavior. In his book *Human Nature and Conduct* Dewey argued persuasively that much of what men attribute to human nature should be ascribed to habit. The great evils of society (for example, war) are due to "social conditions rather than an old and unchangeable Adam."[2] Yet Dewey did not totally abandon the idea of human nature. He granted that there are "ineradicable impulses" in man, although these can be directed into many channels.[3] In the 1929 Preface to the book originally published in 1921, he warned against overlooking "the basic identity of human nature amid its different manifestations."[4] Still later he declared his "faith" in human nature.[5]

Since we have already sampled the discussion of this issue among the psychologists (Chapter IX) and the cultural anthropologists (Chapter X), I shall here look at one of its great contemporary secular formulations in the controversy between Jean-Paul Sartre and Albert Camus. These two brilliant and eloquent Frenchmen, after their early cooperation, came to strenuous disagreement on this issue.

Sartre speaks for the existentialist, Faustian faith that man is whatever he wills himself to be. Values are not given—by God, nature, or the social hierarchy. Instead, "we invent values." "The value of it [life] is nothing else but the sense that you choose."[6] In a statement that has a lineage going back to Pico della Mirandola, although it derives more directly from Nietzsche, Sartre declares: Man "is what he wills. . . . Man is nothing else but that which he makes of himself."[7] So firmly does Sartre believe this that he comes to the famous proclamation: "We are unable ever to choose the worse. What we choose is always the better. . . ."[8] (I shall quote the rest of that sentence in the next paragraph.) All this is subject to the qualification that the choice is made in "good faith"—that it is a genuine choice and not a cowardly flight from choice.

What man genuinely decides is good, not because it meets the external criteria of good, but because man by his decision makes it good.

Such a doctrine might seem to be so obviously mistaken, so plainly opposed to Sartre's own denunciations of his opponents (whether European anti-Semites or American politicians and generals) that many have wondered whether Sartre can really mean what he says. It turns out that he can mean it only by adding a curiously Kantian universalism: "What we choose is always the better; and nothing can be better for us unless it is better for all."[9] While denying that there is "a universal essence that can be called human nature," Sartre affirms that "there is nevertheless a human universality of *condition*," constituted by "all the *limitations* which *a priori* define man's fundamental situation in the universe."[10]

This is a considerable concession. But it is not enough for Camus, who came to believe that there is a universality of human fraternity and of moral demand upon man. The Sartrean ethic, he concluded, encouraged too much arbitrariness and expediency—often for the sake of some distant good but at the cost of immediate compassion.

Camus gave his answer to Sartre—or, rather, his answer to Ivan Karamazov and the entire tradition that led to Sartre—in his most massive book, *The Rebel*, first published in France (*L'Homme Révolté*) in 1951. The book is an analysis of rebellion and an argument that "a human nature does exist."[11] "If there is no human nature," says Camus, "then the malleability of man is, in fact, infinite. Political realism, on this level, is nothing but unbridled romanticism, a romanticism of expediency."[12]

Rebellion, Camus maintains, is inherent in man, yet constantly threatens man with its excesses. "But rebellion, in man, is the refusal to be treated as an object and to be reduced to simple historical terms. It is the affirmation of a nature common to all men, which eludes the world of power."[13] It is that "nature common to all men" that Camus increasingly celebrated until the day of his untimely death.

At the same time that Camus was writing *The Rebel*, he was completing his novel *The Plague*, which is the powerful affirmation of a tragic humanism. I call it a tragic humanism because it is a compelling confession that "there are more things to admire in men than to despise,"[14] joined to an acknowledgment that the plague (representing the antihuman forces both outside and inside man) "never dies or disappears for good," but only lies dormant and "bides its time, awaiting its day of reemergence."[15]

Theology, insofar as it is concerned for dialogue with philosophy and culture, has an interest and even a stake in a debate like that between Sartre and Camus. But the comparable theological debate takes a somewhat different form. The Biblical sources do not characteristically describe God and man in terms of nature and substance. They record the acts of God and man.[16] Since God has a consistent character and men act in certain typically human ways, there is no necessary violation of the Biblical materials to talk of the nature of both. But this is to use a level of abstraction a step removed from the immediate data. Therefore, contemporary theology debates the issue of the nature of man, but not in the same way as theology does.

We can look at the issue in the long discussions between two giants of American theology, friends closely allied in many a cause, yet very different in theological styles: Paul Tillich and Reinhold Niebuhr. In the earlier parts of their careers the two were considered rather close to each

other theologically, but their debate became public with
the publication of Tillich's *The Courage to Be* (1952) and
Niebuhr's *The Self and the Dramas of History* (1955).

For Tillich, man understands himself and truly becomes himself only as he discovers that his existence is
rooted "ultimately in the structure of being itself."[17] This
means that ontology is prior to ethics. Hence, Tillich sees
the issue of human life in "the ontological act of the self-
affirmation of one's essential being."[18] The source of human anxiety is the awareness of finitude and nonbeing.
"The basic anxiety, the anxiety of a finite being about the
threat of nonbeing, cannot be eliminated. It belongs to
existence itself."[19]

The Self and the Dramas of History can be read as Niebuhr's reply to Tillich. Niebuhr believes that "the unique
capacity for freedom of the human person" makes it impossible to fit the self into any of the classic ontologies.
Hence he defines the self, not in terms of its structure of
being or its participation in the encompassing structure
of being, but in terms of its dialogues. "The self is a
creature which is in constant dialogue with itself, with its
neighbors, and with God, according to the Biblical viewpoint."[20] Similarly he interprets human communities in
"dramatic historical" terms rather than in terms of "ontological fate."[21] Above all, he insists, "the Christian faith
does not derive its idea of love from the idea of 'being.' "[22]

These differences between two influential interpreta-
tions of man are important. Yet equally important is the
way in which the two converge in certain insights characteristic of the new humanism.

Thus Tillich, with all his emphasis on ontology, is determined not to lock man into any rigid structure of
being. He affirms the reality and importance of freedom.
In a statement almost Niebuhrian in style, he says:

In every encounter with reality man is already beyond this encounter. He knows about it, he compares it, he is tempted by other possibilities, he anticipates the future as he remembers the past. This is his freedom, and in this freedom the power of his life consists.[23]

Niebuhr, on the other hand, reaches toward Tillich when he rejects exaggeration of freedom or reduction of freedom to capriciousness. Personality, he says, "is characterized by both a basic structure and a freedom beyond structure."[24] Concerned though he is to affirm freedom, he criticizes the Nietzschean and Sartrean doctrines in which "the freedom and the uniqueness of the individual is asserted in defiance of any systems of consistency or universal meaning."[25]

The debate about man's nature and his freedom continues within the Christian doctrine of man. Theological humanism currently is emphasizing man's freedom, against the ideas of a fate or a fixed nature that chain man in. Yet it insists upon a shared humanity, known ethically and existentially. Roger Mehl seeks to unite both these emphases. The Christian believes, says Mehl, that "we are not fixed in a nature, in a completed thing, in a substance. . . . The future remains, with all its newness, full of contingence and surprise." Yet, he continues, the "ultimate meaning" of that future is known, and "all men are recapitulated in Christ (whether they know it or not)."[26]

The discussion of this issue will continue. For the moment it is enough to say that the contemporary Christian doctrine of man opts for the open future rather than for a fixed nature of man. Yet it knows that it is useless to talk of humanism unless we have some notion of what it is to be human.

I shall return to this issue in the final chapter of this book.

CHAPTER XIV

Is Man a Religious Being?

Arnold Toynbee, the famed historian (although an atypical one), has said: "Religion is an essential element in Human Life which cannot ever be ignored or repressed for very long at a time."[1] But Dietrich Bonhoeffer, the theologian, earlier wrote, "We are proceeding towards a time of no religion at all: men as they are now simply cannot be religious any more."[2]

These two statements represent a major debate about the nature of man. Is he inherently a religious being or is he not? Is secular indifference to religion a true evidence of man's real feelings, or is it a deceptive veneer?

In the context of the new humanism, religion is a controversial topic. A theologian today is as unlikely to praise religion as a politician is to condemn it. But there are obvious problems of definition here. Exactly what is the relation between the religion the theologian criticizes and the religion the politician acknowledges? Or between the religion that Toynbee finds man unable to repress and Bonhoeffer finds him unable to practice truthfully?

To get at the answer I must pull together some threads that I have been spinning throughout this book. I have earlier (Chapter V) described the contemporary zest for a worldly Christianity. On this issue Bonhoeffer hails Karl

Barth, who first "called the God of Jesus Christ into the lists against religion."[3] Bonhoeffer is echoing Barth when he declares that Christ is "the Lord of the world" rather than "an object of religion."[4] He is attacking the religious ghetto—whether this be the ghetto of "inwardness" (discussed in Chapter XI), the ghetto of metaphysical speculations removed from the concrete experience of men, or the ghetto of a church that insulates men from the full joys and pains of humanity. All these are in Bonhoeffer's mind when he calls for a "religionless Christianity."

In another phrase Bonhoeffer refers to religion as "the garment of Christianity." It is an unnecessary garment that "has had very different aspects at different periods."[5] Here we may wish that Bonhoeffer had had the opportunity to elaborate his ideas and to answer some perplexing questions. Is it possible to isolate a pure Christianity from all humdrum garments? Only the most docetic Christianity can avoid human accouterments, and Bonhoeffer certainly does not want a docetism. The word that became flesh in ancient Galilee constantly seeks enfleshment in other societies, whether they be imperial, feudal, or industrial. It is quite appropriate that its garments take on "different aspects at different periods." But, as Bonhoeffer sees with such painful clarity, the risk and often the fact is that men then tend to value the garments above the faith. That is why the theological criticism of religion is always necessary.

In all these criticisms of religion, Bonhoeffer is moving in the mainstream of contemporary theology—a mainstream whose course he has done much to direct. But the more controversial point, the point most important for the doctrine of man, is a somewhat different one. It is the idea that secular history has now brought man to the point where he no longer wants or needs religion. Barth had not made this point—and still does not. Bonhoeffer's stimulating and puzzling affirmation is that modern man, come of age, does not have the religious feelings or the sense of need that have haunted religious man through the ages.

The issue is joined in Bonhoeffer's debate with Tillich, a debate thoroughly worth exploring. Tillich is a philosopher-theologian who speaks of religion unabashedly.

Tillich's appreciation of religion is the more noteworthy because he could criticize it as devastatingly as anyone else. Long before the currently fashionable theological polemics against religion, Tillich wrote an essay (1922) called "Overcoming the Notion of Religion Within the Philosophy of Religion."[6] Twenty years later he wrote: "The first word . . . to be spoken by religion to the people of our time must be a word spoken against religion."[7] Yet in championing the "passion toward the profane," the "passion for the secular,"[8] Tillich always profoundly loved religion, provided he could define it. In a characteristic statement he said: "Religion is the state of being grasped by an ultimate concern . . . which qualifies all other concerns as preliminary and which itself contains the answer to the question of the meaning of our life."[9] Again, "Religion, like God, is omnipresent; its presence, like that of God, can be forgotten, neglected, denied. But it is always effective, giving inexhaustible depth to life and inexhaustible meaning to every cultural creation."[10]

Is it possible that the religion Tillich appreciates and the religion Bonhoeffer attacks are so different that there is no argument? We might say that both affirm faith in God and both reject the idolatries and superficialities of conventional religion. Thus a bit of linguistic analysis might remove the conflict.

But that is too easy a solution, especially since Bonhoeffer specifically criticizes Tillich's attempt to give the world a religious interpretation that the world does not want.[11] When Bonhoeffer associates religion with metaphysics and inwardness,[12] when he questions the validity of talking about the "borders of human existence,"[13] and when he opposes "the existentialist philosophers and the psychotherapists" who are "secularized off-shoots of Christian theology,"[14] he seems to have in mind specifically Tillich's theological method and doctrine.

Is Bonhoeffer really maintaining that man in his maturity can live without the "ultimate concern" and "dimension of depth" that are so important to Tillich? Sometimes it seems so. I began this chapter by quoting: "Men as they are now simply cannot be religious any more." They no longer need support in failure or help in weakness. Even death and sin are no longer serious "borders of life."[15]

Yet there is clearly another side to Bonhoeffer. I have already (Chapter XI) mentioned his poem, "Who Am I?" There is the description in another poem of God who feeds the human body and spirit, who forgives Christians and unbelievers.[16] There is the discipline of prayer and Bible study maintained in prison, the confession that only in the "spirit of prayer" can the reconstruction of theology be carried through.[17] There is the confidence in the "guiding hand" of God in the last months in prison.[18]

In these and like statements Bonhoeffer is the best critic of those who too dogmatically schematize him. His own writing remains penetrating, disturbing, and cryptic.

This ambivalence toward religion persists in many theologians who appreciate the legacy of Bonhoeffer. Bishop Robinson in his spectacularly influential *Honest to God* acclaims Bonhoeffer's "religionless Christianity." Yet for his own theological reconstruction he curiously turns to

Tillich on just those themes which had provoked Bonhoeffer's challenges of Tillich.[19]

Hans Hoekendijk has offered varied judgments on the religious nature of man. In 1952 he objected to the description of modern man as "post-religious." Many "familiar religious phenomena," he granted, were disappearing. But he noted "just as emphatically the process of a growing sacralization, which constantly makes us stand in amazement at new 'transpositions and displacements of the sacred.' "[20] But in 1961 he stated his own theological conviction (akin to Barth's and Bonhoeffer's) that religion has "had its day." "After the cross, there was no more future for religion; it was filed in the Past Historic."[21]

Most interesting of all is Harvey Cox's struggle with this issue in his scintillating book, *The Secular City*. One of his major theses is that religious man is an anachronism. "Secularization simply bypasses and undercuts religion and goes on to other things. . . . The age of the secular city . . . *is* an age of 'no religion at all.' "[22] Like Bonhoeffer he links religion with metaphysics and finds that both are "disappearing forever."

Modern pragmatic man, says Cox, does not ask religious or "borderline" questions:

Life for him is a set of problems, not an unfathomable mystery. He brackets off the things that cannot be dealt with and deals with those that can. He wastes little time thinking about "ultimate" or "religious" questions. And he can live with highly provisional solutions. . . . He does not ask religious questions because he fully believes he can handle this world without them.[23]

Cox makes clear that he approves this pragmatism and secularization. It would be hard to find a more forthright challenge to Tillich's beliefs about the inalienably religious quality of human existence.

Yet Cox can sound a contrapuntal theme. Sometimes he finds that man does raise something like the religious question:

Thus we meet God at those places in life where we come up against that which is not pliable and disposable, at those hard edges where we are both stopped and challenged to move ahead. God meets us as the transcendent, at those aspects of our experience which can never be transmuted into extensions of ourselves. He meets us in the wholly other.[24]

Much of that paragraph, if we omit the phrase, "the wholly other," might have been taken from Paul Tillich's descriptions of religion. In some such way, then, the new humanists join their theological criticism of religion with an awareness that man is—if the phrase is carefully defined—a religious being.

An interesting confirmation comes from Paul Goodman, whose lively mind I have drawn upon earlier in this book. This thoroughly contemporary, ecclesiastically uninhibited critic of our culture has commented on the religious concerns of college students:

In my observation, it is an error to say that the present-day young are not interested in religion in a metaphysical sense. It would be odd if this were so, in the transitional and revolutionary state of our world, facing as it does a literal apocalypse. A solid agnosticism, even more than a solid faith, requires a stable world on the march to a rational paradise —a world one might have believed in when John Dewey was a boy.

Since youth are denied any such confidence, says Goodman, they are forced into religious inquiry. Consistent with the secularizing theologians, Goodman sees the political and religious acts merging. Hence there may be a disappearance of some of the familiar cultural signs of religion. But he adds, "Chaplains who say that students are interested in action but not in religion should ponder the implications of the student word 'commitment.' "25

The religious awareness today does not always wear conventional labels. Perhaps, as Nathan Scott suggests, a novelist like Ernest Hemingway—although a modern Stoic rather than a Christian—gives us "a sense of man as a creature who is, willy-nilly, the *homo religiosus*"—a man sensitive to "the absurd" and the "power of blackness," yet "moved by intimations of the Sacred."26 To recognize such a religious awareness in Hemingway requires, of course, a livelier religious imagination than many churchmen can claim.

As interesting as the question, Is man a religious being? is the related question, Why is the evidence so hard to locate? One reason is that the religious experience of our time will be different from such experiences of other ages, to the extent that contemporary man has a different self-awareness. Inquirers should not expect to find in our culture the precise clues to the meaning of religion for man that they find in the medieval world or the Reformation. The more perplexing reason is that contemporary man is so confused and so adept at deceiving himself that he finds it extremely hard to interrogate his own experience and come up with honest answers. Often he is not sure, in his divided being, whether he is a nonreligious being, pretending for the sake of piety and memory to have a sense of need and a faith, or whether he is disturbed by ultimate questions and an ultimate concern, which he keeps hidden because he desperately wants to be contemporary.

The evidence on the religious nature of man is not all in. But thus far it makes difficult any conclusion that man has left the religious question behind.

CHAPTER XV

How Confident Has Man a Right to Be?

John Bennett, analyzing a set of documents prepared for the Geneva Conference on Church and Society, saw "a mood of greater hope for man's historical future than has often been present in ecumenical circles, certainly a mood that is ready for radical changes."[1] He found mixed causes for the new ethos. Among the nations that had recently won independence, there was a sense of expectancy. Among other nations he suspected that affluence "may have more influence on theology than theologians like to admit."

Bennett's own assessment of the change appears in the following words:

The optimism of the days of the Stockholm Conference in 1925 and the ideological confidence of more recent periods are no longer possible. Yet there are grounds for expectancy and even for hope. . . . Theologians are inclined to see the human in man reasserting itself in spite of much brainwashing.[2]

At the same time Paul Abrecht, drawing upon his experience of many years in the ecumenical movement, pointed to the historical forces that are contributing to "an emerging world society." A "Christian interpretation of this new historical dynamism" is, he said, "the great challenge to Christian social thinking in the years ahead."[3]

Dynamism and hope, although not identical, are surely related. When the World Council of Churches met in Assembly in 1954 at Evanston, the theme was "The Christian Hope." For many participants this meant an eschatological hope—a hope for redemption "beyond history," which offered some motive force and security but not much expectation for improvement within history. By Geneva, 1966, the hope was far more historical in the context of an eschatology constantly imminent and operative in history. Where once utopianism had been the enemy, now lethargy and consecration of a rigid *status quo* were the targets.

Sounds of Optimism

We have already (Chapter IV) noted the cosmic optimism of Teilhard de Chardin. The current generation of new humanists is less inclined to metaphysical speculation on the grand scale, more oriented to the present cultural and political scene. Here, despite their awareness of a world in recurrent crises, they are issuing frequent declarations of hope.

American theology is especially interesting in this regard. America has characteristically been a land of confidence. Now some of its theologians, emerging from the chastening influence of the neo-orthodox criticism of optimism, are reasserting this traditional hopefulness.

Thus Harvey Cox, although he does not go so far as to reinstate the old doctrine of inevitable progress, comes close to it. He finds the processes of secularization to be inevitable and irreversible. And secularization is very close to progress. In it God is releasing men to maturity. This means hazards for men, but it means primarily hope. Secularized, mobile man is less tempted by idolatry than his forebears; he is liberated to freedom and responsibility.[4] The Christian sees "all of history since the coming of Jesus as the beginning of a new regime." The forces that "cripple and corrupt human freedom" have not been annihilated, but they no longer "have the power to determine man. Rather, man has the power and responsibility to rule over them and use them in responsibility before God."[5]

The most explicit statement of the new confidence comes from William Hamilton, who throws aside the usual theological inhibitions and actually uses the word "optimism." Hamilton has not always been so hopeful. In a 1964 article he very nearly renounced faith and hope in favor of love. In America, he surmised, "the theologian today and tomorrow is a man without faith, without hope, with only the present, with only love to guide him."[6] Two years later hope had returned—with a bang. Hamilton declared himself on the side of "a willingness to count on the future and a belief in its real improvement."[7]

His reasons came from an impressionistic sampling of some evidences from the arts, the social sciences, and current history. The method is evident in his title: "The New Optimism—from Prufrock to Ringo." He was contrasting the timid melancholy of T. S. Eliot's character of 1917 with the "mood of celebration and rejoicing" in the Beatles' film, *A Hard Day's Night,* of 1964. Hamilton might have noticed that 1917 was also the year of Edgar Guest's *A Heap o' Livin'* and that *A Hard Day's Night* appeared between the stage version (1962–1963) and the screen version (1966) of *Who's Afraid of Virginia Woolf?* Obviously Hamilton—or if not Hamilton, somebody else —could write another essay entitled "The New Pathos— from Eddie Guest to Eddie Albee."

Hamilton suggests that "tragedy is culturally impossible"[8] today—and proposes that the reason is the "death of God." He might have noted Joseph Wood Krutch's famous essay of 1929, "The Tragic Fallacy." Krutch, too, thought that tragedy had become impossible, but not despair. Tragedy, said Krutch, depended on the "assumptions that the soul of man is great, that the universe (together with whatever gods there may be) concerns itself with him and that he is, in a word, noble."[9] Because "a light has gone out in the universe," the theater can show misery but not tragedy. Krutch in 1954 (*The Measure of Man*) modified his outlook in the direction of a chastened hopefulness, but not an exuberant optimism.[10] Meanwhile the theater, in the works of Harold Pinter, Samuel Beckett, Jean Genet, and Peter Weiss, demonstrated that the mood of the Beatles no more dominated the arts in the 1960's than had the mood of the marvelous Marx brothers in the generation before.

When Hamilton turns to the social sciences and politics, his data are equally impressionistic. He relies on the gallant but brief confidence of the civil rights movement and on Lyndon Johnson's Inaugural Address of 1965 in a way that appears strange just a few years later. Fifteen months after Hamilton's essay on "The New Optimism," James Reston published his regular column under the heading "Washington: The New Pessimism."[11] If Reston is right, "the old optimistic illusion that we can do anything is giving way to doubt, even to a new pessimism that maybe the problems of the nations, the cities and the races are beyond our control." To the extent that this is a move from "rhetoric" to "reality," Reston approves it. My point in quoting Reston is not to refute one mood with another, but to suggest that man's self-understanding had better not stake too much on any momentary mood.

Among the new optimists the most ecstatic and also the most provincial is Thomas Altizer, who unites faith in progress, American messianism, and a sanctificationist ethic. The assurance of progress is a modified Hegelian dialectic that drives history forward in apocalyptic hope. The American messianism—which Altizer would want sharply distinguished from official White House and State Department messianism, despite obvious similarities—is the evocation of "America's original promise of a universal historical liberation of humanity."[12] The sanctificationist ethic—"The Christian is liberated from the alien power of the moral imperative by virtue of his life in Christ"[13]—is rather close to Billy Graham's solution to the racial problem of some years ago, before Graham discovered the relevance of public laws and social institutions to prejudice.

It is easy to discredit the new optimism by pointing to its most extravagant expressions. It is harder and more important to assess the meaning and validity of the tough-minded demands for action and hopes for success that are becoming more prominent in our era.

There are no authenticated experts at reading the dynamics of our turbulent history. Erich Fromm heralds the possibility of *The Sane Society* and Chad Walsh writes *From Utopia to Nightmare*.[14] William Hamilton acclaims "not an optimism of grace, but a worldly optimism,"[15] while Malcolm Muggeridge says: "The curtain, indeed, is falling, if it has not already fallen, on all the utopian hopes which have prevailed so strongly for a century or more."[16] Paul Goodman combines both notes in a stimulating way, writing his portentous criticisms of contemporary society,[17] yet commending utopian thinking.[18]

What is happening is the reappraisal of the hopes—so buoyantly announced, so disastrously rebuffed—of the

eighteenth-century Enlightenment. When Hamilton confesses "an increased sense of the possibilities of human
action, human happiness, human decency in this life,"[19]
something in all of us responds. But it was not always so.
In most centuries of human history men assumed that
they lived under a fate which decreed that the future
would be about like the past. Jewish messianism brought
mankind the idea of a dynamic history and an open future
in which God would transform the quality of life. The
Christian gospel brought a sense of life "between the
times"—between the time of a transformation actually
wrought in Christ and a consummation of that transformation still to come. But later orthodoxy sluiced off that
dynamism into otherworldiness and left men living in a
largely static history.

The Enlightenment reinstated something like the Christian hope in a secularized way. As Carl Becker put it, the
philosophers of the eighteenth century "demolished the
Heavenly City of St. Augustine only to rebuild it with
more up-to-date materials."[20] Or, as Crane Brinton has
said, the really new belief of the Enlightenment was "the
belief that all human beings can attain here on this earth
a state of perfection hitherto in the West thought to be
possible only for Christians in a state of grace, and for
them only after death."[21]

The new theological optimism has followed an intellectual pilgrimage from twentieth-century neo-orthodoxy
through the skepticism of Ivan Karamazov to the confidence of the eighteenth-century *philosophes*—although,
certainly in the case of Hamilton, with a far more attractive sense of humor than the *philosophes* exercised. Sometimes (as in Harvey Cox and Arend van Leeuwen) the outcome includes elements of Comte's nineteenth-century

world view, with its law of progress through three stages of history.

I have no intention of discrediting an idea by showing its lineage. Many an idea of the past deserves a new hearing and new formulation. The only advantage in recognizing the history of an idea is to see it in perspective.

The eighteenth century had a vision and a confidence of man's power to improve his world. The immature forms of that hope were destroyed, for at least three reasons. (1) The objective events of history—the revolutions, tyrannies, and calculated cruelties of the twentieth century—were the exact opposite of the eighteenth-century descriptions of "posterity." (2) Marx and Freud, with help from history, showed man's skill in using his rational competence as a weapon of his partisan interests and irrational purposes. (3) The actual achievement of some of the utopian hopes of the past—widespread educational opportunities, higher standard of living, use of elections and democratic institutions, devices of mass communications, social security, greater leisure and life expectancy —has brought bitter as well as beneficent effects.

To all this blasting of the pathetic hopes of the past, the new humanism must respond by reasserting some of the inherited visions. The Enlightenment was right in seeing that the future will be different from the past. There are human possibilities for the present generation unknown to any earlier generation.

For the first time in history man has the technical capacity to eliminate starvation and physical hunger, to do away with the desperation of poverty and economic insecurity. Man can diminish drudgery and open up to everyone the possibility of enjoyments of leisure once known only to a few. Man can give everyone access to education. He can assuage the ravages of disease and the bodily pain of finitude.

A faith that expresses itself in love will welcome these opportunities and make the most of them. It may be more or less optimistic, depending upon the historical situation, but its resolution will not depend on its optimism. A humanistic faith will never use a transcendent hope to evade the responsibility for improving the human condition now. It may find that its transcendent hope sustains efforts in the midst of tragedy and pathos.

SUFFERING AND TRAGEDY

To that tragedy and pathos I must now give attention. Christian faith—in fact, all profound faith, within whatever religion or irreligion it operates—has traditionally had a double relation to man's expectations. It has called man to responsibility, raising his aspirations beyond the prosaic goals his society sets for him and inspiring him to noble achievements. Simultaneously it has reminded man of his mortal incompleteness, of the limits within which the person and society function, of the need for a fulfillment that somehow transcends the here and now.

In the New Testament both themes speak from the same Paul. "I can do all things in him who strengthens me." (Phil. 4:13.) There is the faith that breaks barriers in aspiring confidence. "If for this life only we have hoped in Christ, we are of all men most to be pitied." (I Cor. 15:19.) There is the awareness of mortality and the fragmentary quality of a human existence that is always inadequate in itself.

In Johannine language this is the world that God so loved that he gave his son for it, the world in which the Word became flesh and in which God thereby blessed all flesh (John 3:16; 1:14–16). Yet this is the same world that crucified Christ, the world that Jesus warned would hate his disciples (John 15:19).

The new humanism reminds Christians, who have too often forgotten the fact, that this world is God's world and man's home. It reminds Christians to be grateful for their humanity and appreciative of the humanity of their neighbors. It warns them that to despise humanity, whether in themselves or in others, is heresy. It speaks to man's aspirations. It must also, if it is to be a mature humanism, take account of man's frailty.

Christian thought has always recognized human weakness in two forms: first, man's creatureliness; second, his sin. Here I shall consider his frailty. In the following chapter, I shall come to his sin.

As creature, man is finite, yet unique among created beings. Sometimes in his *hubris* he forgets that he is not God. He may with Nietzsche aspire to become God; or he may, without giving God a thought, simply set out to do whatever God is supposed to do.

The new humanism wants to rescue man from frustration and humiliation, to free man from political and religious subjection. It calls him to responsibility. Sometimes it forgets that man is a creature.

William Hamilton recalls the night in his backyard when he helped his son identify some constellations for a school assignment. The father remembered his own boyhood feeling of awe and dependence when he looked at the stars. But the son, "a full citizen of the modern world," had a quite different feeling. His question was, "Which are the ones we put up there, Dad?"[22]

The answer might seem obvious. "We" put up mighty few of them. And the ones we put up are tiny trinkets in the vastness of interstellar space. And, as one of the American astronauts put it, "Man will never conquer space.

At most he will learn to move around in it." But to Hamilton his son's question represented the spirit of technological man, rightly impressed with his own "mastery, control and power." (Or perhaps this conclusion merely shows one of the occupational hazards of writing theology for *Playboy*.)

In a somewhat different vein Harvey Cox writes: "For the Bible, there are no powers anywhere which are not essentially tameable and ultimately humanizable. . . . The taming of the powers means that man is invited to make the whole universe over into a human place."[23] Such a statement is puzzling in the same sense as the similarly ambitious metaphysical statements of Teilhard de Chardin, on which I have commented above (Chapter IV). Is there not a major strain in the Bible asserting that God's inscrutable purposes encompass more than man and that the creation is more than "a human place"? Is there not an unanswerable folk wisdom in the comment of Saul Bellow's Augie March, "You do all you can to humanize and familiarize the world, and suddenly it becomes more strange than ever"?[24]

When Charles West suggested that Cox had neglected the meaning of suffering, forgiveness, and grace, Cox made a gracious and thoughtful reply acknowledging that he had skimped the "element of tragedy, of depth, judgment and mystery." These, he said, belong with the "celebrative mood" of the gospel.[25]

The Czech theologian, J. M. Lochman, combines the notes of confidence and of warning—perhaps because he lives in a culture where the processes of secularization have frequently taken an overtly anti-Christian form. Hence his caution may be all the more pertinent to our society, where secularization may tolerate or even patronize Christianity. Lochman sees plainly what the American theologian may easily forget, that the Christian lives always as "a stranger and sojourner" in culture. His definition of the double temptation for the Christian is utterly relevant to the affluent society that America is creating. The one temptation is that of a "theological giddiness" in which Christians "lose theological independence" and let their gospel "simply become adapted to the new situation and ideology." The opposite temptation is to reject the new developments of the secular society out of longing for the transient world of the past.[26]

The meaning of Lochman's position for the issue of Christian confidence and hope is, I suppose, that the Christian identifies himself with all those human hopes which enhance the life of man, that he rejoices in every gain for the human cause, that he enjoys the lightheartedness and spontaneity which are part of human life. At the same time he perceives the narrowness and shallowness of many human purposes and the insecurity of many achievements. In "abundance and want" (Phil. 4:12) he maintains hope.

In the profound words of Hans Hoekendijk, ours is a world in which "the Christian hope will have to be proclaimed so convincingly that every other expectation is exposed as Utopia, every other hope as *false* hope." Men "often pass by the grave of every human expectation." Then "hope will have to be learned again out of the bankruptcy of all human hope."[27] When men face the question of "whether human existence is still livable," they may learn to recognize "the desert as the promised land."[28]

God has made this world so alluring that men can sometimes enjoy its oases without noticing its deserts. But in the nature of human existence, the confidence that flourishes in the oasis is rarely adequate unless it can also endure the desert.

CHAPTER XVI

What About Sin?

Humanism always means some esteem for man and his potentialities. The new humanism, I have been saying, sometimes displays a striking optimism. What has happened in theological humanism to the Christian awareness of sin?

The past generation in theology rediscovered sin. It did so in a remarkable historical situation. Much of modern culture and theology had forgotten about or tried to obscure the reality of sin; yet man was demonstrating his capacity for sin in terrible ways. So theologians, starting with assumptions of man's goodness, discovered and exposed sin with an awesome fascination and a polemical zeal.

The more recent theologians did not need to discover sin. They were told about it in their theological education; they read about it constantly in the press; they experienced its cost in war. What they discovered was that, in the midst of sin, man has capacities for nobility and dignity. They were more impressed by their discovery than by what they had started out taking for granted.

But sin, obviously, persists. The new humanism must take account of it.

At Emory University's convocation on "America and the Future of Theology" in November of 1966, a dramatic confrontation on this issue took place. Thomas Altizer expressed his jubilation in American messianism and the coming of the new age. Then Rabbi Richard L. Rubenstein, replying, said that he missed the needed note of anguish. He agreed with Altizer about "the death of God as a cultural event." But he rejected "too quick a dance of joy at the great funeral." Then the rabbi reminded the Christian of "the old Augustinian-Calvinist notion of original sin," describing it as a theological insight "on target."[1] Throughout two days Rabbi Rubenstein impressed the predominantly Christian gathering with the facts of the concentration camps of the twentieth century and the vicious nature of the human sin that is sometimes subdued but never eliminated from life.

Perhaps it required a Jew, a member of an obvious minority, to remind Christians of the insights that they recognized when they were a minority but often forget now that they can fade so easily into the cultural landscape. But Christians know about sin—both as its victims and as its perpetrators. They have to come to terms with it in their lives and in their doctrine of man.

Recent theology has to some extent revised its inherited ideas about sin. Its response to sin is—as most items in a doctrine of man are expected to be—paradoxical.

One side of the paradox is the indignation at the behavior of man that is part of the humanistic concern for man. The more anyone values man, the more he must protest against his mistreatment.

It is hardly necessary to emphasize that ours is an age of protest. Never have nations waged war with such internal questionings and opposition as since World War II. Rarely have men seen so keenly the brutal and brutalizing power of racial hostility. The possibility of affluence for all has brought sensitivity to the sin that consigns some to poverty. Mass society provokes protests against the manipulation and depersonalization of people. Youth, in particular, seeing the gap between pretense and performance, protests against hypocrisy and cries for honesty. In all these protests is an awareness of sin and guilt.

The other side of the paradox is an intense concern with human possibilities. The certainty that the future will be different from the past rouses the hope, anguished or cheerful, that it will be better than the past. The very moral sensitivity that awakens protest is itself an evidence of some unquenched good in man. There are signs of renewed utopianism among those who have seen so many improbable things done that they refuse to believe that anything cannot be done. Especially among the youthful nations and within the youth culture in many societies is this yearning expectation for a better future. The paradox is perhaps most evident in the intimate relation between the frequent trust in the future and the distrust of whatever forces or establishments control the present.

All this may seem to be simply another statement of the traditional paradox in Christian doctrine: Man, created in the divine image, is nevertheless a sinner. But every generation must rediscover and rearticulate this paradox in the light of its own experience. Contemporary theology, stirred by deep intuitions of man's creative and destructive powers, is struggling to clarify its insights.

In the current reformulation of the doctrine of man and his sin, a frequent question concerns the specific character of sin. Did the theology of the recent past overemphasize the sin of pride and neglect the sin of sloth?

For example, did so penetrating a thinker as Reinhold Niebuhr successfully expose man's temptation to play God and overlook his sheer inertia?

If we go back to the days of the social gospel, we find Walter Rauschenbusch saying, "The most important and persistent obstacle of progress is the conservative stupidity and stolidity of human nature."[2] The generation just after Rauschenbusch saw sin less as stolidity than as dynamic, vicious lust for power. Today many Christians are reclaiming the insight of Rauschenbusch.

John Bennett has often commented that Reinhold Niebuhr showed a brilliance in analyzing the dynamic sins of man, the sins of conquest or of tenacity in clinging to privilege, but gave no comparable attention to the sins of indifference. Bennett's criticism is an affectionate one. He observes that Niebuhr himself is so incapable of apathy that he cannot give the traditional sin of sloth a prominent place in his doctrine.

Niebuhr's doctrine of sin—still the comprehensive, intricate formulation against which younger theologians test their wits—recognizes the issue. Man in the anxiety of his mingled finitude and self-transcendence seeks escape from insecurity and the dizziness of freedom. He can try to escape in two ways. The first is the proud and desperate effort to become more than human—that is, to establish a security that finite man can never really possess. The second is to sink into a less than human existence by denying his freedom and smothering his distinctively human aspirations.[3] Of the two, Niebuhr typically emphasizes the former. He tears the camouflage from the foolish pride and idolatries of men—of big tyrants who try to make themselves masters of the destiny of other men on the grand scale, and of petty tyrants who gloat over cheap triumphs within the family or the small community. He analyzes such sin in individuals and in nations, races, and social classes.

He says less about those who are buried in the struggle. He often takes their side in the conflict. He has worked with the labor movement and in many a political organization or committee trying to help the weak. He has said that "most men perish in weakness, frustration and confusion," that "their lives are determined by circumstances," that they suffer "from frustrated and unfulfilled desires."[4] But this is his less characteristic theme. By and large he has little to say about the experience that some Christians are finding in the ghettos—where frustration is so oppressive that it is hard to awaken people to action; where the development of some pride, at least self-respect, is painfully difficult; where apathy day in and day out is a greater enemy than the fanaticism that occasionally breaks out; where progress depends less upon shattering vain ambition than upon overcoming hopelessness. He has less to say about defeatism than about vanity, about indifference than about fanaticism.

Certainly Niebuhr's doctrine and ethic speak realistically to many of the most critical issues of our day. Some of the sentences in Senator Fulbright's *The Arrogance of Power* are interchangeable with sentences in Niebuhr's Gifford Lectures. "Power confuses itself with virtue and tends also to take itself for omnipotence. Once imbued with the idea of a mission, a great nation easily assumes that it has the means as well as the duty to do God's work."[5] The statements are verifiable by analysis of public documents. It is sometimes said that the United States government today is not arrogant—that it is confused, unsure of itself, unconfident of its purposes. But that is no refutation of Fulbright. The insecure are often the most arrogant.

Hans J. Morgenthau, George Kennan, and Arthur M. Schlesinger, Jr., have used insights specifically derived from Niebuhr to interpret the errors of American foreign policy. Edmund Stillman and William Pfaff have shown, with occasional references to Niebuhr, how America has been self-deceived by pride and moral fervor into misunderstanding its role in history, whether seeking in isolation to remain superior to the rest of the world or aiming by military might to set right a sinful world.[6]

Hence the new humanism will be wise to remember Niebuhr's analysis of pride, even as it investigates the problems of inertia and defeatism that have concerned Niebuhr far less.

On one other issue contemporary theology is rethinking the capacity of man to cope with his sin. This is the issue of using rational and technological ingenuity to moderate some of the traditional conflicts of power.

One of the fondest hopes of modern man, from the Enlightenment through the heyday of pragmatic liberalism, was that reason would tame fanatic furies and reduce the conflicts in life. Theology sometimes took up the hope. But in the last generation theology showed convincingly that in sinful man reason operates as the instrument of self-interest and partisan group interest. Rather than the neutral adjudicator of power conflicts, reason—very often, at least—is a weapon in the power struggle.

The new humanism wants to give reason another chance. The remarkable powers of technology change the traditional human conflicts in two ways.

The first is that the destructive potentialities of nuclear weapons have given the nations with greatest military power an awareness of the limitations of power. Reason can—sometimes—see the foolishness of destroying an enemy if the consequence is self-destruction. In one way the effectiveness of reason is, therefore, literally unprecedented. Repeatedly nations, in the face of temptations that might in other times have been irresistible, have held back from unleashing their most destructive weapons. As I write this, I have no way of knowing how persuasive it will be by the time these words are printed. The subservience of reason to interest is still evident in the painful difficulties of achieving even modest restraints on weaponry or national sovereignty. To moderate the escalation of the arms race is a major achievement. To deescalate the arms race or the worst international conflicts usually seems beyond any power of reason.

The second change is in the ability of man to devise scientific and technological solutions to some of the problems that have required hard decisions and provoked conflicts in the past. The most obvious example is affluence. Conceivably technology can answer the old question, Who shall go hungry? by saying, Nobody. Instead of fighting over how to cut the economic pie, men may make a big enough pie that they will care less about the minutiae of the cut. Thus in the early days of President Johnson's plans for a "Great Society," Walter Lippmann pointed out the unique feature of the program. It was to be financed out of increasing production. For the first time in history production was growing at such a rate that a society could improve the lot of the poor, raise the quality of education, rebuild cities, expand medical care for everyone—without taking anything away from anybody. Here was the opportunity to gain moral ends without any sacrifice.

Out of this situation has risen a new breed of administrators, who are not primarily power brokers but technicians. Their aim is to resolve power conflicts by application of economic and social scientific skills.

All of us had better wish them success. The human race needs every advantage it can find. I believe that technology and the social sciences give us the possibility of resolving many problems for which the past simply had no answers. Although we are far from the achievement, the human race actually can eliminate starvation. It can solve some of its age-old problems.

But the use of technology and the social sciences takes place within a power structure. Here Niebuhr's familiar theme is undeniable: power blocs will rarely reform society on their own. They must be confronted with power before they will change. Every technological answer to the problems of the metropolis runs into obstacles of power: Where will the tax money come from? How will the privileges of suburbs be maintained? Who will pay for elimination of pollution? What will happen to rents and rental income? Which ethnic groups will feel threatened? What will happen to states rights?

In fact, technology makes possible, perhaps demands, new concentrations and constellations of power. There is the military-industrial complex that President Eisenhower warned against in his "Farewell Address." There are the powers of manipulation in control of the hidden persuaders and rulers of mass communications. Again I refer to Walter Lippmann, who argues rather persuasively that man simply has not learned how to make democratic institutions work in a technological society.[7]

There are further evidences. The "Great Society" ran into the war in Vietnam, and it quickly became evident that the poor would pay for the war. Neither prosperity nor reason has solved the race problem. Change has come only when the oppressed could muster sufficient power to create a situation of conflict, in which they could hurt both the self-interest and the previously unconcerned consciences of people in power. Affluence has improved the economic status of most of our society, but the 20 percent of the desperately poor remain economically almost as bad off as ever and culturally even more isolated from the society than previously. On a world scale the gap between rich and poor increases, while more people die of starvation than ever before.

A humane and technological reason remains a precious gift to man. No humanist has any right to despise it. But technological advance does not eliminate moral struggle. Those who cherish reason had better realize its frailty.

Describing "the new optimism," William Hamilton says: "It faces despair not with the conviction that out of it God can bring hope, but with the conviction that the human conditions that created it can be overcome, whether those conditions be poverty discrimination, or mental illness."[8] I am reluctant to oppose such obviously fine idealism. I agree that human effort and wisdom can solve some problems. But in our human history problems persist, and solutions frequently bring new problems.

I am particularly perplexed when Hamilton associates his confidence with a move "from the 'pessimism' of Paul to the eschatological optimism of the synoptics."[9] Is not the heart of the Synoptic Gospels the passion narrative? Does not the Christian life always have a cruciform quality—because man is frail and man is a sinner? These questions the new humanism must continue to face.

Chapter XVII

Who Is Man, and What Is Humanism?

The final question is one that has been lurking in every chapter of this book. I have skirted it often and have made brief forays in the direction of an answer. Now I must look at it directly. Who is man, and what is humanism?

The current theological passion for humanization sometimes fails in clarity for one obvious reason. The word "human" has both an empirical and a normative sense, and the gap between the two is immense. In the empirical sense, anything people do is human. Human behavior is a mixed bag, containing all that the newspapers report or suppress, all that priests and psychiatrists hear in clerical or secular confessionals, all that people think or do. In this sense humanization is unnecessary. Men are already humanized, because humanization gets its definition from whatever men are and do.

In the normative sense, the human is assumed to be good. The word implies some ideal or some recognition of a humanity that is not simply the factual discovery of men's feelings, thoughts, and actions. It judges that many acts which, empirically speaking, are human, are in a profounder sense subhuman or antihuman. It requires an act of the ethical imagination.

Empirically speaking, the Nazi destruction of six mil-

lion Jews was human. It was not done by inhuman tigers
or impersonal computers. People—men and even women
—did it. We can call it inhuman only if we have some
evaluation of what it is to be human.

In the current theological vocabulary, the language of
humanism and humanization has largely replaced the language of nature and natural law. I think it is a better
language, but it retains a similar problem. The traditional
concept of natural law in ethics often confused an empirical and a normative meaning. Now a similar confusion
persists in the ethics of humanism and humanization.

Aristotle, one of the founders of classical humanism,
saw the problem:

For man, when perfected, is the best of animals, but when
separated from law and justice, he is the worst of all; since
armed injustice is the more dangerous, and he is equipped at
birth with arms, meant to be used by intelligence and virtue,
which he may use for the worst ends. Wherefore, if he have
not virtue, he is the most unholy and the most savage of
animals, and the most full of lust and gluttony.[1]

Aristotle was more sure than most modern men about
how man's arms were "meant" to be used or what man was
meant to be. Our world hears a confusion of voices on
such issues. Hence humanism, per se, offers few guides for
living. Yet it assumes that, in the midst of all the human
activities constantly happening, something valuable is
going on—and something threatening. Humanism becomes meaningful when man has some revelation of the
possibilities of human life.

THE HUMAN AND THE IMPERSONAL;
THE HUMAN AND THE INHUMAN

In trying to understand what is genuinely human, there
is some help in a double distinction: first, between the

human and the impersonal; second, between the human and the inhuman.

The distinction between the human and the impersonal is the easier to define. In this respect most people have a fairly sure sense of what it is to be human. Here I return to Dietrich Bonhoeffer: "For many to-day man is just a part of the world of things; the experience of the human simply eludes them."[2]

To humanize life is to refuse to make people into things. It is to protest with Dostoevsky against turning man into a piano key. It is to reject with Kierkegaard the temptation to renounce personal responsibility and sink into the mass. It is to acclaim with Reinhold Niebuhr man's mysterious freedom. It is to cherish with Martin Buber the richness of I-Thou relationships. It is to join Bonhoeffer in appreciation of the opportunity to be a man, without succumbing to the sentimental "cult of the human."

This assertion of the human against the impersonal, so important in all human history, has its special significance in our history. Society is telling some people that they are not important because they are less competent than machines. It is telling others that they must subject their selfhood to the demands of organization. The new humanism responds by raising a flag for man. It replies insistently that computers and organizations are made by men, that their function is to serve men.

The answer to Karel Capek's *R.U.R.*, to Huxley's *Brave New World*, and to Orwell's *Nineteen Eighty-Four* will not be the destruction of machines or bureaucracy. It will be the valiant effort to turn the machines and bureaucracies to human purposes. "Our concern," says Rabbi Abraham Heschel, "is not how to worship in the catacombs but rather how to remain human in the skyscrapers."[3]

Any such humanization requires both imagination and

struggle. Kenneth Keniston sees three options before contemporary society: "whether to attempt to turn the clock
back so as to 're-create' a bygone society in which our
modern alienations did not yet exist, whether to 'continue'
the present triumphant march of a technological process
which has created these same alienations, or whether to
begin to define a new vision of a society whose values tran-
scend technology."[4] When the issue is put that way, almost
anybody will opt with Keniston for the third possibility.
But, as he shows, the usual response to the third challenge
is to assign some more money to hunting the same technical answers that enhance the second option.

To humanize our world, against the depersonalizing
forces so active in it, is a challenge both alluring and in-
timidating to modern man. But increasingly he senses the
issue.

Now I turn to the second and even more profound
issue. Humanization in the first sense, the sense of rescu-
ing man from depersonalizing forces and liberating him
for his human potential, heightens the urgency of understanding the second distinction—between the human and
the inhuman. Common language, when it refers to an inhuman action, means not that it is impersonal but that it
is cruel, vicious, ruthless. Such actions are empirically
thoroughly human, but they are an offense against the humanity of both the victim and the perpetrator.

The problem is that human nature, as we know it, is
at war with itself. Man is, in the words of William Faulkner, this "stalemate of dust and desire." The desires—all
of them human—fight one another and try to transmute the
dust. Man, says biologist Julian Huxley, is the small being
in whom "the vast evolutionary process . . . is becoming
conscious of itself"; he is the torchbearer "of advance in
the cosmic process of evolution."[5] Man, says anthropologist

Loren Eiseley, is "the lethal factor," fearing truth, fearing himself, threatening the very life process on the globe, his home.[6]

Alfred North Whitehead in a vivid phrase said that human reason includes the reason that Ulysses shares with the foxes and the reason that Plato shares with the gods.[7] That was a wise comment, but perhaps unfair to the foxes.

In the last century Ivan Karamazov made a harsher judgment on man:

People talk sometimes of bestial cruelty, but that's a great injustice and insult to the beasts; a beast can never be so cruel as a man, so artistically cruel. The tiger only tears and gnaws, that's all he can do. He would never think of nailing people by the ears, even if he were able to do it.[8]

More recently Konrad Lorenz, in his much publicized book *On Aggression,* has said that only two species of animals systematically destroy other beings of the same species: brown rats and men.[9] Lorenz finds man's aggressiveness deeply rooted in his phylogenetic inheritance. Ashley Montagu, in a stinging rebuttal, maintains that "far from being innate, man's aggressiveness is a learned form of behavior."[10] The interesting and disturbing point is that, in either case, man's destructiveness turns out to be a distinctively human trait, not a characteristic widely shared by animals.

When humanists make their plea for the humanization of man, they plainly do not mean to urge man to heighten his destructive propensities—although these are distinctively human. They mean something quite different. They are employing an ethical awareness of human nature and its possibilities against a merely empirical measurement of humanity. In doing so, they are surely right.

The trouble is that man with his immense gifts and conflicting abilities is rarely sure what he wants to be or what he means by becoming human. It is this uncertainty that produces the variety of types of humanism.

CLOSED AND OPEN HUMANISM

One divergence within humanism is represented by what I shall call the closed and the open types of humanism. In closed humanism man is militantly loyal to mankind simply because, within the context of the universe, mankind represents "our side." Man wants to survive and uphold human values in about the same way that a pack of wolves wants to survive and maintain wolf-values—although, presumably, man does so with more imagination and foresight than the wolf. The nonhuman world is the field of conquest; its only value is its value for man.

An open humanism sees man in his wider setting. It recognizes his kinship with nature, and it acclaims values that have no utilitarian advantage for man. Thus John Dewey—I mention Dewey because he was generally regarded as a humanist and was intensely critical of traditional religions—objected to "militant atheism" with its "lack of natural piety" and its "exclusive preoccupation" with "man in isolation." (For the record, I should quickly add that Dewey made much the same charge against "supernaturalism.") "A humanistic religion," wrote Dewey, "if it excludes our relation to nature, is pale and thin, as it is presumptuous, when it takes humanity as its object of worship."[11]

Recent years have seen a paean of protests against the crude, exploitative humanism of a commercial culture. When profit-greedy interests justify the destruction of redwood forests or the indiscriminate spreading of DDT by claiming to set "human values" above the values of trees and wild life, almost anybody becomes cynical about this style of "humanism."

Biologists have often led the protest. They have called attention to the devastating effect of many human acts upon ecology—the marvelously intricate relations between organisms and their environment. So geneticist Bentley Glass has said that just as man must enlarge his horizons from individual to family to nation to the brotherhood of man, he must go still farther. "Man as a species is a member—only one of many members—of a terrestrial community and an even greater totality of life upon earth. . . . In this sense, coexistence is not only necessary but also right."[12] Microbiologist Catherine Roberts has objected to certain types of experimentation with animals, not only because they inflict unnecessary cruelty but also because by degrading animals they degrade men. On humanistic grounds she affirms that "Hebrew, Buddhistic, Socratic, and Christian teachings were on an infinitely higher ethical level than the dicta of a humanism that foresees the subversion of teleological attitudes and which teaches that the Good Life means to increase secular bliss and ensure its survival."[13]

Architects increasingly complain against the adoration of the bulldozer and the wrecking of natural landscapes for the sake of human construction. Artur Glikson of Tel Aviv is one of many who believe that a crude exploitation of land is part of "an increasing alienation of man from his environment."[14] Since Frank Lloyd Wright, an increasingly articulate group of architects has urged that human constructions work with rather than fight against nature, and an economically oriented society has occasionally heeded them.

In the future perhaps even economics will recognize the

danger of a closed humanism. Kenneth Boulding, economist and social philosopher, foresees an increasing resem-
blance between the planet and a spaceship:

We have to visualize the earth as a small, rather crowded
spaceship, destination unknown, in which man has to find a
slender thread of a way of life in the midst of a continually
repeatable cycle of material transformations. In a spaceship,
there can be no inputs or outputs. . . . Up to now the human
population has been small enough so that we have not had to
regard the earth as a spaceship. We have been able to regard
the atmosphere and the oceans and even the soil as an
inexhaustible reservoir, from which we can draw at will and
which we can pollute at will. There is writing on the wall,
however.[15]

In the future, says Boulding, "Western expansionism and
aggressiveness and the concept of man as the conqueror
of nature" may have to learn from the wisdom of the East,
which "has never had any illusions about being able to
conquer nature, and has always regarded man as living
in a somewhat precarious position, as a guest of doubtful
welcome, shall we say, in the great household of the natural world."[16]

All these voices, some of them representing belief in
God and some not, point to the limitations of a closed
humanism. Arnold Toynbee does the same thing, with
quite specific reference to religious faith. Toynbee's thesis
is that man's worship of his own power has through the
ages been his favorite religion. This religion takes three
characteristic forms: the idolization of a parochial community, which has destructive, antihuman implications;
the idolization of an ecumenical community or world society, which is better but is still stifling to the human
spirit; and the idolization of a self-sufficient philosopher,
which is also confining and perhaps sterile. All these forms
of worship, says Toynbee, have two errors: (1) "Man is

not God," and (2) "the worship of human power prevents the worshipper from finding the right attitude towards Suffering." Through the cost of suffering man gains "a glimpse of a God who is Love as well as Power, and who is not a deification either of Human or of Non-Human Nature, but is the deliverer of these and all His creatures from the evil of self-centredness to which every creature is prone."[17]

Something like the logic of Toynbee's argument appears in theological form in H. Richard Niebuhr's book, *Radical Monotheism and Western Culture,* the final book published during his lifetime. He finds "the religion of humanity" to represent an admirable impulse, insofar as it is a protest against "the little faiths in little gods," which attract most men. But in the end it is too introverted, too confining. More inclusive, says Niebuhr, is Albert Schweitzer's "reverence for life," since its loyalty "goes out to the whole realm of the living and every member of it." But it, too, is exclusive. So Niebuhr describes a radical monotheism that excludes no "realm of being from the sphere of value." "A radical monotheism would include reverence for the dead, and that not simply because they were once alive; it would include also reverence for beings, inorganic perhaps, perhaps ideal, that though not living claim the wondering and not exploitative attention of us other creatures that have the will-to-live."[18]

In this discussion of closed and open forms of humanism, I have avoided stating the issue in terms of non-theistic and theistic humanism—although that distinction deserves attention. Its limitation, as both Toynbee and Niebuhr show, is that many theistic forms of humanism are as idolatrous as the more avowed worship of a nation or community. Hence, at this stage of the analysis, it is more helpful to distinguish between the closed humanism, in which man meets his world in the mood of conquest or plunder, and the open humanism, in which he acknowledges some grateful appreciation to the sources of his own being and to the nonhuman environment that nourishes his life, evokes his wonder, and that endures beyond the limits of his historical existence.

SELF-CONFIDENT AND GRACEFUL HUMANISM

There is a second comparison, as important as that between closed and open humanism. It is not easy to name the next two types, but I am calling them self-confident and graceful humanism. The first lives by a confidence in man's capacity to realize and enjoy his potentialities; the second lives by a trust in a grace given to man. I do not think the two are entirely opposed or even separable, but there is a difference worth thinking about.

Rudolf Bultmann, in a lecture at the University of Chicago in 1951, analyzed the intimacy and the tension between "Humanism and Christianity." Of the classical humanism, coming from the Greco-Roman tradition, he said: It "expresses the conviction that man by virtue of his spirit is able to shape his life in freedom and to subject to himself the world in which he has to live his life; and furthermore, that through his culture man can make the world his home." By contrast, he continued, "the Christian faith expresses the conviction that man is not his own master, that this world is an alien country to him, and that he can gain his freedom from the world only with the help of divine grace, which is freely given to the world from the beyond."[19]

The theological humanism that has developed so swiftly

in recent years is more "worldly" than the faith that Bultmann describes. It is reluctant to call the world "alien,"
and it looks for divine grace to give the Christian freedom
for as truly as freedom from the world. In these respects
it combines the two traditions Bultmann describes, as in
his judgment Western culture often has done. Bultmann
finds the two allied against nihilism, totalitarianism, and
the many antihuman movements of our time.

Yet he finds the distinction still important. The humanist "actualizes his real self in ongoing progress, in
ceaseless labors on himself, in the process of culture (*pai-
deia*). . . . He carries within himself the sperm from which
his real 'I' progressively develops."[20] In Bultmann's description of humanism, I should point out, there is no
denial of God, nor is there any necessary affirmation of
God. Western humanism, in most of its tradition, has
affirmed God, in one sense or another, but that is not the
major point.

Christian faith depends in a quite different way upon
God, who is "always the hidden one and the coming one."
As Bultmann continues, "With this transcendent God man
has communion only in openness to the future, which is
not at man's disposal or under his control. . . . This readiness to enter the darkness of the future confidently is
nothing else but readiness for my transcendent self which
stands before me. . . . The Christian life as 'life-out-of-the-
future' does not mean the actualization of an idea of man
but rather a 'life-out-of-the-future' which can be seized
only in the moment of decision."[21]

Bultmann does not make this comparison for polemical
purposes. He asks his hearers to find "the genuine, dynamic balance" between the two faiths, to acknowledge
the difference, yet to "remain true to the humanistic and

the Christian traditions, so that their powers may become effective once more in our culture."[22] Even so, there is no doubt that Bultmann wants to take his stand with Christian faith.

Let us, therefore, look at someone who represents the humanistic belief as ardently as Bultmann represents the Christian. Erich Fromm offers this definition: Humanism is "in simplest terms, the belief in the unity of the human race and man's potential to perfect himself by his own efforts." Such humanism includes great varieties. Humanists may or may not believe in such articles of faith as the goodness of man or the existence of God. "But," says Fromm, "all Humanists have shared a belief in the possibility of man's perfectibility, which, whether they believed in the need for God's grace or not, they saw as dependent upon man's own efforts."[23]

Like Bultmann's, Fromm's is an irenic definition. He is not excluding Christians from the humanist faith; in fact, he specifically includes Kierkegaard, although he excludes Luther. I need not stop here to inquire how well he understands Kierkegaard or Luther, or whether he would be likely to include Bultmann as a humanist. Likewise I need not quibble over the term "perfectibility" and whether it means improvement or the potential attainment of perfection. I would rather point out that almost every Christian today finds some attractiveness in Fromm's definition, and most would probably like to be included in it, if they could have the privilege of defining a word or two.

Yet the issues posed by Bultmann and Fromm point to an important, if almost indefinable, distinction. In Christian faith man is really not trying to perfect himself. He is not trying to fulfill all his potentialities.

I am not saying that Christians do not do these things or that there is something evil in trying. What I am saying is that this is not the life of faith. Likewise, I am not saying that in faith men, to use the familiar caricature, simply wait—in agony or complacency—for God to pull them out of their sins, or rejoice in the midst of the world's wretchedness because they have been saved.

What I am saying is that in Christian faith life is a response to a grace which has seized man, shaken him, and blessed him in Jesus Christ. This grace shows him a self and a potentiality that he does not otherwise know that he has. This is why H. Richard Niebuhr has said that the Christian man is not so much the maker (artificer or goal seeker) or the law obeyer (the disciplined citizen) as the responder, "the responsible self." He is "man-the-answerer, man engaged in dialogue, man acting in response to action upon him."[24]

The Christian man understands his life as a gift, which is both a blessing and a perilous opportunity. He accepts freedom as a gift—a peril and a joy. He does not know or spend much time worrying about whether he is perfecting himself; life is too full of needs and opportunities calling for response. He recognizes a compelling call, yet responds to it with spontaneity.

This faith can be called a humanism, because it is a response to a man—to Jesus of Nazareth, whom Christians call the Christ—and because it prompts the Christian to live out his life as man or woman. But I call it graceful humanism, because it is response to a gracious gift, including the gift of human existence itself. It means a grateful life, which combines appreciation of and discontent with the world, with society, with the self. It is not so much a matter of looking within oneself for the norms of humanity as it is a perpetual awakening to new possibilities and new graces that are given.

In a similar way graceful humanism is a gracious humanism in relation to the neighbor. It has some trouble with that great, yet often glib, humanistic phrase, "the dignity of man." It knows how often men renounce their own dignity and stifle the dignity of others. So perhaps it remembers with Helmut Thielicke the traditional belief in an "alien dignity,"[25] that ineradicable gift that persists in man even when he does not know how to claim it. Or perhaps it sees with Paul Lehmann the sanctity of the individual, who may or may not evidence dignity.[26] Whatever its language, it recognizes in the fellowman a neighbor and a brother.

And yet—something is wrong with this description. Even when it is said far more persuasively than I can say it, there is a false note in it. The reason is that experience often does not fit the categories. The world knows humanists—classical humanists, secular humanists, Marxist or existentialist humanists—who live with grace, as though their lives were a response to a gracious gift. And the world knows Christians—Catholic, Protestant, or sectarian Christians—who live in arrogance over their virtue or in crabbed obedience to unpleasant duty.

To this, Christian faith must say: Of course. The Christian life is a response to grace as well as a working out of grace, and men can make a mess of the response. On the other side of the question, Christians should never be so foolish as to say that the divine grace they have met in Christ works only among men who know about Jesus or believe in him. Indeed, "the grace of our Lord Jesus Christ" is "the love of God the father" and "the fellowship of the Holy Spirit." Nobody, certainly no Christian,

can prescribe the workings of God or dictate the operations of the Spirit, who blows where he wills (John 3:8).
There would be a blasphemy in claiming that Christians
are better than other people or that Christians have the
last word on what it is to be human.

But this reasoning, too, is not the last or only word.
Humility as well as pride can be a game. Christians, in
renouncing the pride and exclusivism of some of their
forefathers, do not help the situation by saying in blithe
modesty that faith really does not matter. It is the Christian faith that in Jesus Christ men have seen a new revelation of divine love and human possibilities. To that they
respond in gratitude.

I can sum up the issue by quoting two short phrases
side by side. But before I do so, I must warn against any
premature judgments. I am not trying to win a propagandistic victory by showing the moral superiority of Christianity to secular humanism. I am trying to get at the answers to two questions: Who is man, and What is humanism?

So here are the phrases. One is from Erich Fromm:
"man for himself."[27] The other, which I have already used,
is from Dietrich Bonhoeffer, describing Jesus: "the man
for others."

Immediately I must repeat my warning: Any premature
judgment here will miss the point. Fromm no less than
Bonhoeffer insists that the heart of ethics is love. His book
Man for Himself is an argument against the popular psychology of adjustment and against ethical relativism. The
man whom Fromm wants to be and act "for himself" is
not individualistic man or tribal man but universal man.

So the two statements are not simply opposed in sullen
hostility. On the other hand they are not simply a happy

combination. Together they approach the core of the issue of human nature.

To live for others, Christian faith confesses, is in some profound way to realize oneself. But it is not a calculated method whereby service of others becomes the means of self-aggrandizement or self-realization. That can be one of the nastiest forms of egoism. Nor is it a reversal of the means-end process, making self-destruction a means toward self-fulfillment. Such self-destruction is simply that —self-destruction.

In a Christian humanism man discovers his own humanity via the grace he knows in Jesus Christ, via a free obedience and an obedience that frees, via a sharing in the death and resurrection of Christ. He is not making the concentrated and resourceful effort to be himself; he is celebrating the gift of life and freedom.

Man can never claim this gift in lonely defiance—although there is much in our world to defy. He can never receive it in slavish obedience—although there are calls that he must obey.

He can never hoard the gift in lonely isolation—although there are times for solitude. He can never enjoy it when lost in the crowd—although he must learn to lose himself.

The influence of Christian faith upon life may sometimes be invisible, with no consequent embarrassment because it is not an inspirational banner for the world. At other times it may become highly visible, with no shame over its nonconformity. As J. M. Lochman puts it, the Christian man "is, in the full meaning of the phrase, a 'contemporary,' a man among men." But this same man is an ex-centric man in an ex-centric community of faith.[28] In a similar spirit, Robert Spike once wrote: "To be human is not to be natural. To be a man in the fullest sense is to be disturbed and intrigued by what we see in Christ."[29]

Pontius Pilate put it still more simply, although in his cynicism he did not know what he was saying. "Here is the man!" (John 19:5.)

The man Jesus has the compelling grace that calls out of others the recognition of God and of their brothers. As in him men meet God and their brothers, they come also to self-recognition. That is the meaning of Christian humanism.

Notes

CHAPTER I
THE DYNAMICS OF CHRISTIAN THOUGHT ABOUT MAN

1. The story is attributed to the German biologist, von Uexhall, by the Strasbourg biologist, M. Klein. See Gordon E. W. Wolstenholme, ed., *Man and His Future* (Little, Brown and Company, 1963), p. 288.

CHAPTER II
FROM OXFORD TO GENEVA

1. The words are those of J. H. Oldham in his summary of the conference. Dr. Oldham was chairman of the Research Commission doing preparatory work for the conference and was one of the guiding figures in the conference. See *The Churches Survey Their Task: The Report of the Conference at Oxford, July 1937, on Church, Community and State* (London: George Allen & Unwin, Ltd., 1937), p. 48.

2. Published in Reinhold Niebuhr, *Christianity and Power Politics* (Charles Scribner's Sons, 1940), Ch. 16, "The Christian Church in a Secular Age."

3. See *The New Humanist*, Vol. VI, No. 3 (May–June, 1933), pp. 2 f.

4. Frederick J. E. Woodbridge, *An Essay on Nature* (Columbia University Press, 1940), p. 125.

5. "Epilogue," in John C. Bennett, ed., *Christian Social Ethics in a Changing World* (Association Press, 1966), p. 371.

6. *Ibid.*, pp. 141, 142.

7. *Ibid.*, p. 229. Dr. Chandran quotes these words from the document *Christian Participation in Nation Building* (Bangalore, 1960), p. 304. This book came out of the joint studies of the National Christian Council of India and the Christian Institute for the Study of Religion and Society.

8. In Z. K. Matthews, ed., *Responsible Government in a Revolutionary Age* (Association Press, 1966), p. 336.

9. J. M. Lochman, in Bennett, ed., *Christian Social Ethics in a Changing World*, p. 245.

10. J. M. Lochman, "How Can the Church Contribute to the Transformation of Society?" address at Conference on Church and Society, July 22, 1966.

11. Helmut Gollwitzer, in Matthews, ed., *Responsible Government in a Revolutionary Age,* p. 58.

12. Paul Lehmann, *Ethics in a Christian Context* (Harper & Row, Publishers, Inc., 1963), p. 14 *et passim.*

13. Robert Burns, "Man Was Made to Mourn," stanza 7.

CHAPTER III
REASONS FOR THE NEW HUMANISM

1. *Pastoral Constitution on the Church in the Modern World,* Dec. 7, 1965, Part 9. In Walter M. Abbott, S.J., ed., *The Documents of Vatican II* (Guild Press, Inc.; The America Press; Association Press, 1966).

2. Paul Goodman, "Student Chaplains," *The New Republic,* Vol. 156, No. 1 (Jan. 7, 1967), pp. 29–31.

3. Winston Churchill, address of June 18, 1940.

4. M. M. Thomas, opening address, Conference on Church and Society, Geneva, Switzerland, July 12, 1966.

5. Decision in the Macintosh case, written by Justice Sutherland, 1931.

CHAPTER IV
SOME LEADERS IN THE CHANGE

1. Paul Tillich, *Perspectives on 19th and 20th Century Protestant Theology* (Harper & Row, Publishers, Inc., 1967), p. 5.

2. Karl Barth, *The Epistle to the Romans,* tr. from the sixth edition by Edwyn C. Hoskyns (London: Oxford University Press, 1933), Preface to the First Edition, p. 2.

3. *Ibid.,* Preface to the Second Edition, p. 10.

4. Karl Barth, "No!" Answer to Emil Brunner in Karl Barth and Emil Brunner, *Natural Theology*, tr. by Peter Fraenkel (London: Geoffrey Bles, Ltd., 1946). The specific references are from pp. 79, 87, 88, 89.

5. Karl Barth, *The Knowledge of God and the Service of God*, tr. by J. L. M. Haire and Ian Henderson (London: Hodder & Stoughton, Ltd., 1938), p. 232.

6. Karl Barth, *The Church and the Political Problem of Our Day* (Charles Scribner's Sons, 1939), p. 58.

7. Karl Barth, "How My Mind Has Changed," *The Christian Century*, LXVI: 298 (March 9, 1949).

8. Karl Barth, "The Christian Message and the New Humanism," in *Against the Stream: Shorter Post-War Writings, 1946–52*, ed. by Ronald Gregor Smith (Philosophical Library, Inc., 1954), pp. 183–201.

9. Karl Barth, in *The Humanity of God*, tr. by John Newton Thomas and Thomas Wieser (John Knox Press, 1960), pp. 37–65.

10. *Ibid.*, p. 43.

11. *Ibid.*, pp. 46, 49, 50, 51.

12. "A Letter from Karl Barth," *The Christian Century*, LXXV:1510 (Dec. 31, 1958).

13. Barth, *The Humanity of God*, p. 65.

14. Dietrich Bonhoeffer, *Prisoner for God*, ed. by Eberhard Bethge; tr. by Reginald H. Fuller (The Macmillan Company, 1954), pp. 166, 167, 168. The British edition and a later paperback edition in America have the title, *Letters and Papers from Prison*.

15. Robert Spike, *To Be a Man* (Association Press, 1961); Ronald Gregor Smith, *The New Man: Christianity and Man's Coming of Age* (London: SCM Press, Ltd., 1955).

16. Bonhoeffer, *Prisoner for God*, p. 179, from the "Outline for a Book."

17. *Ibid.*

18. *Ibid.*, pp. 182–183.

19. Reinhold Niebuhr, *The Nature and Destiny of Man*, 2 vols. (Charles Scribner's Sons, 1941, 1943). The paperback edition was published in 1964 with the same pagination as the original, but with a new preface. It is the edition quoted here.

20. *Ibid.*, Vol. II, pp. 60–61.

21. *Ibid.*, Vol. II, pp. 109, n. 6; 123.

22. *Ibid.*, Vol. II, pp. 204–212.

23. *Ibid.*, Vol. I, p. viii. *Man's Nature and His Communi-*

ties (Charles Scribner's Sons, 1965), pp. 23–24.

24. Reinhold Niebuhr, *Man's Nature and His Communities*, pp. 15–16.

25. Reinhold Niebuhr, *The Nature and Destiny of Man*, Vol. I, p. viii. *Man's Nature and His Communities*, p. 109.

26. Reinhold Niebuhr, *Man's Nature and His Communities*, pp. 109–110, 117–119.

27. *Ibid.*, pp. 113–117.

28. Jacques Maritain, *True Humanism* (Charles Scribner's Sons, 1938). The book originated in lectures delivered in Spain in 1934. It appeared in French under the title *L'Humanisme intégral* in 1936.

29. *Ibid.*, p. 63. This is not the place to ask whether Maritain understood Barth adequately. But Maritain wrote prior to Barth's change of direction, described earlier in this chapter.

30. *Ibid.*, p. 69.

31. *Ibid.*, p. 131.

32. *Ibid.*, p. 105.

33. Jacques Maritain, *Le Paysan de la Garonne* (Paris, 1966).

34. Charles Moeller, "The Church in the Modern World," address at the Conference on Church and Society, Geneva, July 16, 1966.

35. *Ibid.*

36. Pierre Teilhard de Chardin, *Letters from a Traveller, 1923–1955* (London: Collins Fontana ed., 1967), p. 225; letter of Jan. 12, 1941.

37. *Ibid.*, p. 297; letter of Oct. 30, 1954.

38. Pierre Teilhard de Chardin, *The Phenomenon of Man* (Harper Torchbooks, Harper & Brothers, 1961), p. 180.

39. *Ibid.*, pp. 232, 244.

40. *Ibid.*, p. 284.

41. *Ibid.*, p. 290.

42. *Ibid.*, p. 307.

CHAPTER V
THE CELEBRATION OF THE SECULAR

1. See p. 33 above.

2. Reinhold Niebuhr, *Christianity and Power Politics*, p. 222.

3. Bonhoeffer, *Prisoner for God*, pp. 167, 168 (July 18 and 21, 1944).

4. *Ibid.*, pp. 146–147 (June 8, 1944).
5. Albert Camus, *The Rebel* (Vintage Books, Random House, Inc., 1956), p. 306. Originally published in French in 1951.
6. Bonhoeffer, *Prisoner for God*, p. 142 (May 25, 1944).
7. *Ibid.*, p. 145 (June 8, 1944).
8. *Ibid.*, p. 146 (June 8, 1944).
9. *Ibid.*, p. 164 (July 16, 1944).
10. *Ibid.*, p. 183 (Aug. 21, 1944).
11. *Ibid.*, p. 184 (Aug. 21, 1944).
12. *Ibid.*, p. 123 (April 30, 1944).
13. *Ibid.*, p. 136 (May 21, 1944).
14. *Ibid.*, p. 139 (May 21, 1944).
15. Friedrich Gogarten, *Verhängnis und Hoffnung der Neuzeit: Die Säkularisierung als theologisches Problem* (Stuttgart: Friedrich Vorwerk Verlag, 1953).
16. See Carl von Weizsäcker, *The Relevance of Science* (Harper & Row, Publishers, Inc., 1964). Cf. Alfred North Whitehead, *Science and the Modern World* (The Macmillan Company, 1925); Herbert Butterfield, *The Origins of Modern Science, 1300–1800* (London: Bell & Sons, Ltd., 1949).
17. The *Report* on the consultation by Charles C. West received rather wide circulation among the constituency of the World Council of Churches.
18. J. C. Hoekendijk, *The Church Inside Out* (The Westminster Press, 1966), pp. 41, 54.
19. Paul van Buren, *The Secular Meaning of the Gospel* (The Macmillan Company, 1963).
20. Harvey Cox, *The Secular City* (The Macmillan Company, 1965), p. 17.
21. Arend Th. van Leeuwen, *Christianity in World History*, tr. by H. H. Hoskins (Charles Scribner's Sons, 1964), p. 332.
22. Ronald Gregor Smith, *Secular Christianity* (Harper & Row, Publishers, Inc., 1966), p. 156.
23. H. D. Wendland, "The Theology of the Responsible Society," in Bennett, ed., *Christian Social Ethics in a Changing World*, pp. 146–147.
24. Hoekendijk, *The Church Inside Out*, p. 189.
25. M. M. Thomas, "Modernisation of Traditional Societies and the Struggle for New Cultural Ethos," address at Conference on Church and Society, Geneva, July 14, 1966.
26. Dietrich Bonhoeffer, *No Rusty Swords*, tr. by Edwin H. Robertson and John Bowden (Harper & Row, Publishers, Inc., 1965), p. 91.

27. Bonhoeffer, *Prisoner for God,* p. 168 (July 21, 1944).

28. Cf. H. Richard Niebuhr, *Christ and Culture* (Harper & Brothers, 1951).

CHAPTER VI
UNEASINESS IN THE BRAVE NEW WORLD

1. Roger Mehl, *Images of Man,* tr. by James H. Farley (John Knox Press, 1965), p. 5.

2. Bertrand Russell, *Has Man a Future?* (Penguin Books, Inc., 1961), pp. 69–70.

3. In the four preceding paragraphs I have drawn upon and revised part of my essay, "Human Responsibility in the Emerging Society," in *Prospective Changes in Society by 1980* (Denver: Designing Education for the Future: An Eight-State Project, 1966).

4. George Orwell, *Nineteen Eighty-Four* (Harcourt, Brace & Co., Inc., 1949). Aldous Huxley, *Brave New World* (Doubleday & Company, Inc., 1932).

5. Aldous Huxley, *Brave New World Revisited* (Bantam Books, Inc., 1960); original edition, Harper & Brothers, 1958.

6. Kenneth E. Boulding and Henry Clark, *Human Values on the Spaceship Earth* (National Council of the Churches of Christ in the U.S.A., 1966), p. 64.

7. John Thompson, reviewing Norman Mailer's play *The Deer Park* in *The New York Review of Books,* Vol. VIII (April 20, 1967), p. 13.

8. Rollo May, "Antidotes for the New Puritanism," *Saturday Review,* March 26, 1966, pp. 19 ff.

9. David Riesman, with Reuel Denney and Nathan Glazer, *The Lonely Crowd* (Yale University Press, 1950).

10. William H. Whyte, Jr., *The Organization Man* (Simon and Schuster, Inc., 1956).

11. Philip Jacob, *Changing Values in College* (Harper & Brothers, 1957), pp. 1, 2.

12. Kenneth Rexroth, "Disengagement: The Art of the Beat Generation," in Gene Feldman and Max Gartenberg, eds., *The Beat Generation and the Angry Young Men* (Dell Publishing Company, Inc., 1959), p. 351. Rexroth's essay was first published in 1957 in *New World Writing,* No. 11.

13. Herbert Marcuse, *One Dimensional Man* (Beacon Press, Inc., 1964), p. 12.

14. Paul Goodman, *Growing Up Absurd* (Random House, Inc., 1960).

15. Kenneth Keniston, *The Uncommitted: Alienated Youth in American Society* (Dell Publishing Company, Inc., 1967).

16. Michael Harrington, "The Mystical Militants," in *Thoughts of the Young Radicals* (a collection of essays from *The New Republic*, 1966).

17. For a description of the international character of the phenomenon, see Herbert R. Lottman, "A Baedeker of Beatnik Territory," *The New York Times Magazine,* Aug. 7, 1966.

18. Text of the Summary, "Report of the President's Commission on Law Enforcement and Administration of Justice," *The New York Times,* Feb. 19, 1967.

19. Jean-Paul Sartre, *No Exit* (1943), in *No Exit and Three Other Plays* (Vintage Books, Random House, Inc., 1955), p. 47.

20. T. S. Eliot, *The Cocktail Party* (Harcourt, Brace & Co., Inc., 1950), p. 98.

21. Paul Tillich, *The Courage to Be* (Yale University Press, 1952), ch. 2.

22. H. Richard Niebuhr, *Radical Monotheism and Western Culture* (Harper & Brothers, 1960), p. 141.

23. Hannah Arendt, *Eichman in Jerusalem,* revised edition (The Viking Press, Inc., 1964). The quoted words are from the subtitle and from p. 288.

24. Carl Sandburg, from address reported in United Press International dispatch from Chicago, Oct. 30, 1957.

CHAPTER VIII

QUESTIONS FROM THE NEW BIOLOGY

1. Kenneth E. Boulding, *The Meaning of the Twentieth Century* (Harper & Row, Publishers, Inc., 1964), p. 7.

2. See Hudson Hoagland, "Potentialities in the Control of Behavior," in Wolstenholme, ed., *Man and His Future,* pp. 306–307.

3. See Isaac Asimov, "Pills to Help Us Remember?" *The New York Times Magazine,* Oct. 9, 1966. Also, dispatch by Harold M. Schmeck, Jr., *The New York Times,* Aug. 6, 1966.

4. Dr. Delgado's experiments have been widely reported in the press. See also José M. R. Delgado, "Brain Technology and Psychocivilization," in Cameron P. Hall, ed., *Human Values and Advancing Technology* (Friendship Press, 1967).

5. Hermann J. Muller formulated his proposals in a variety

of books and articles. The latest revision of them was in a paper, "What Genetic Course Will Man Steer?" read to the Third International Congress of Human Genetics, Chicago, Sept. 10, 1966. Cf. "Genetic Progress by Voluntarily Conducted Germinal Choice," in Wolstenholme, ed., *Man and His Future*.

6. Theodosius Dobzhansky, "Changing Man," *Science*, 155:411 (Jan. 27, 1967).

7. Winston Churchill, *The Second World War*, Vol. III, *The Grand Alliance* (Houghton Mifflin Company, 1950), pp. 23–24.

8. Hudson Hoagland, "Some Biological Considerations of Ethics," in Harvey Cox, Hudson Hoagland, *et al.*, *Technology and Culture in Perspective* (an occasional paper published by the Church Society for College Work, Cambridge, Mass., 1967), p. 15. Hoagland attributes the data to Francis Crick.

9. Boulding and Clark, *Human Values on the Spaceship Earth*, pp. 1–2.

10. Edmund W. Sinnott, *The Biology of the Spirit* (Compass Books, The Viking Press, Inc., 1961; first published in 1955), p. 129.

11. Edmund W. Sinnott, *The Bridge of Life* (Simon and Schuster, Inc., 1966), pp. 96–97, 129–130.

12. *Ibid.*, pp. 193–194.

13. Muller, "What Genetic Course Will Man Steer?"

14. Theodosius Dobzhansky, *The Biological Basis of Human Freedom* (Columbia University Press, 1956), p. 132.

15. Catherine Roberts, *The Scientific Conscience* (George Braziller, Inc., 1967), p. 26.

16. Norbert Wiener, *God and Golem, Inc.* (M.I.T. Press, 1964), p. 73.

17. Dobzhansky, *The Biological Basis of Human Freedom*, p. 132.

CHAPTER IX
A DEBATE WITHIN PSYCHOLOGY

1. Freud had an interesting modesty about his criticisms of religion. "Freud himself felt anything but certain about his position on religion. He had a low opinion of his own atheistic thesis, 'The Future of an Illusion,' and referring to it he once remarked to René Laforgue: 'I've lost my grip.' He also conceded that it was quite conceivable that people with a (religious) philosophy completely opposed to his own might inte-

grate psychoanalytic concepts into their own view of man."
Karl Stern, *The New York Times Book Review*, July 13, 1952.

2. Sigmund Freud, *The Future of an Illusion* (London: Hogarth Press, Ltd., 1928), p. 93.

3. *Ibid.*, p. 92.

4. Philip Rieff, *Freud: The Mind of the Moralist* (Anchor Books, Doubleday & Company, Inc., 1961).

5. Freud, *The Future of an Illusion*, pp. 9, 11.

6. Sigmund Freud, *Civilization and Its Discontents* (Anchor Books, Doubleday & Company, Inc., 1958), p. 58.

7. Sigmund Freud, *The Origin and Development of Psychoanalysis* (Henry Regnery Company, 1955; originally published, 1910), p. 58.

8. *Ibid.*, pp. 56–57.

9. *Ibid.*, p. 58.

10. Freud, *The Future of an Illusion*, p. 93.

11. Freud, *Civilization and Its Discontents*, pp. 99, 105.

12. Seymour Rubenfeld, "Psychiatry and Existentialism," a book review in *The New Republic*, Vol. 154, No. 26 (June 25, 1966), p. 27. See also Rollo May, ed., *Existential Psychology* (Random House, Inc., 1961).

13. Philip Rieff, *The Triumph of the Therapeutic: Uses of Faith After Freud* (Harper & Row, Publishers, Inc., 1966), p. 8.

14. *Ibid.*, p. 62.

15. Erich Fromm, *The Art of Loving* (Harper Colophon Books, Harper & Row, Publishers, Inc., 1962).

16. Erich Fromm, *The Sane Society* (Fawcett World Library, 1967; first published, 1955).

17. Will Herberg, "Freud, the Revisionists, and Social Reality," in Benjamin Nelson, ed., *Freud and the 20th Century* (Meridian Books, The World Publishing Co., 1957), p. 151.

18. Freud, *Civilization and Its Discontents*, p. 62.

19. Fromm, *The Sane Society*, p. 241.

20. Fromm, *The Art of Loving*, p. vii.

21. *Ibid.*, p. 132.

22. Fromm, *The Sane Society*, p. 313.

23. Rieff, *The Triumph of the Therapeutic*, pp. 24–25.

CHAPTER X
ISSUES FROM THE SOCIAL SCIENCES

1. Julian H. Steward and Demitri B. Shimkin, "Some Mechanisms of Sociocultural Evolution," in Hudson Hoag-

land and Ralph W. Burhoe, eds., *Evolution and Man's Progress* (Columbia University Press, 1962), p. 67.

2. John Dewey, *Human Nature and Conduct* (Modern Library, Inc., 1930), p. 91.

3. Karl Barth, *Credo,* tr. by J. Strathearn McNab (Charles Scribner's Sons, 1936), p. 80.

4. Karl Barth, *Church Dogmatics,* Vol. I, Part I, tr. by G. T. Thomson (Edinburgh: T. & T. Clark, 1936), p. 159.

5. Barth, *The Epistle to the Romans,* Preface to the First Edition, p. 1.

6. Robin G. Collingwood, *The Idea of History* (London: Oxford University Press, 1946), p. 47.

7. J. Milton Yinger, *Religion, Society and the Individual* (The Macmillan Company, 1957), Vol. I, p. 58.

8. Steward and Shimkin, "Some Mechanisms of Sociocultural Evolution," in Hoagland and Burhoe, eds., *Evolution and Man's Progress,* p. 68.

9. Crane Brinton, *Ideas and Men* (Prentice-Hall, Inc., 1950), p. 529.

10. Ruth Benedict, *Patterns of Culture* (Penguin Books, Inc., 1946), p. 6.

11. *Ibid.,* p. 7.

12. Ruth Benedict, "Religion," in Franz Boas, ed., *General Anthropology* (D. C. Heath & Company, 1938), p. 628.

13. Herberg, "Freud, the Revisionists, and Social Reality," in Nelson, ed., *Freud and the 20th Century,* p. 155.

14. Albert Salomon, *The Tyranny of Progress* (The Noonday Press, 1955).

15. Howard Becker, *Through Values to Social Interpretation* (Duke University Press, 1950), p. 297.

16. *Ibid.,* p. 296.

17. Donald N. Michael, *The Next Generation* (Vintage Books, Random House, Inc., 1965), pp. 163–164.

18. *Ibid.,* p. 164.

19. *Ibid.,* p. 165.

CHAPTER XI

THE AFFAIR WITH EXISTENTIALISM

1. Tillich, *The Courage to Be,* p. 137.

2. Bonhoeffer, *Prisoner for God,* pp. 123, 125 (April 30, May 5, 1944).

3. *Ibid.*, p. 165.
4. *Ibid.*, pp. 158–159 (July 8, 1944).
5. *Ibid.*, p. 160 (July 8, 1944).
6. Cox, *The Secular City*, p. 74.
7. *Ibid.*, p. 252.
8. Nathan Scott, "Society and the Self in Recent American Literature," in Roger L. Shinn, ed., *The Search for Identity: Essays on the American Character* (Harper & Row, Publishers, Inc., 1964), pp. 106–107.
9. John Updike, "Anxious Days for the Glass Family," *The New York Times Book Review*, Sept. 17, 1961.
10. Reported by Sidney Hyman, "When Washington Reads," *The New York Times Book Review*, Aug. 14, 1966.
11. Eric Hoffer, "The Negro Is Prejudiced Against Himself," *The New York Times Magazine*, Nov. 29, 1964, p. 109.
12. André Dumas, "In Quest of a New Ethic for New Societies," address at Conference on Church and Society, Geneva, July 14, 1966.
13. Marcuse, *One Dimensional Man*, p. 247. Hochhut's play in its English version is called *The Deputy*.
14. C. P. Snow, *The Two Cultures and the Scientific Revolution* (Cambridge University Press, 1959). Cf. *The Two Cultures: And a Second Look* (Cambridge University Press, 1963).
15. Kenneth Keniston, "The Faces in the Lecture Room," in Robert S. Morison, ed., *The Contemporary University: U.S.A.* (Beacon Press, Inc., 1967), p. 328.
16. *Ibid.*, p. 329.
17. *Ibid.*, p. 330.
18. *Ibid.*, p. 332.

CHAPTER XII
RENEWED CONVERSATIONS WITH MARXISM

1. "One of my ancestors signed a covenant in 1639 in Guilford, Connecticut, which contains the phrase 'from each according to his ability, to each as need shall require.'" (Nym Wales, "Old China Hands," *The New Republic*, Vol. 156 [April 1, 1967], p. 14.)
2. I have analyzed this theme in some detail in *Christianity and the Problem of History* (Charles Scribner's Sons, 1953), Ch. V.

3. Daniel Bell, "The 'Rediscovery' of Alienation," *The Journal of Philosophy,* LVI:933–952 (Nov., 1959).

4. Erich Fromm, *Marx's Concept of Man,* with a translation from Marx's *Economic and Philosophical Manuscripts* by T. B. Bottomore (Frederick Ungar Publishing Company, 1961).

5. *Ibid.,* p. 103. This and the following citations are from the translation of Marx.

6. *Ibid.,* p. 151.

7. *Ibid.,* p. 107.

8. *Ibid.,* p. 140.

9. The comments on Garaudy are based on his book, mentioned above; on a lecture delivered widely in America, "Communists and Christians in Dialogue," published in the *Union Seminary Quarterly Review,* XXII:205–212; and on an interview in *Réalités,* Sept., 1966. In the following paragraphs I am repeating parts of my response to Garaudy published in the issue just listed of the *Union Seminary Quarterly Review.*

10. The eminent economist, Paul Samuelson, says: "Non-economists exaggerate the importance of economic factors in shaping the political history of a nation. (Karl Marx was no exception)." (Column in *Newsweek,* May 22, 1967, p. 89.) However, most Christian theology prior to Marx certainly underestimated the importance of economic factors in shaping history—and even theology.

11. Mehl, *Images of Man,* p. 22.

12. Garaudy, "Communists and Christians in Dialogue," *Union Seminary Quarterly Review,* XXII:205. Garaudy does not give the source of his citation, and I have not located it.

13. Roger Garaudy, *From Anathema to Dialogue: A Marxist Challenge to the Christian Churches,* tr. by Luke O'Neill (Herder & Herder, Inc., 1966), pp. 56–57.

14. In the nature of the case it is difficult to offer documentary evidence for what I say in this and the following paragraphs. My sources are news dispatches in the public press, occasional reports in *Religion in Communist Dominated Areas* (a publication of the International Affairs Commission of the National Council of Churches), discussions with Eastern Europeans visiting America or attending ecumenical gatherings in Western Europe, and two visits of my own to Eastern Europe. See also William C. Fletcher and Anthony J. Strover, eds., *Religion and the Search for New Ideals in the USSR* (Frederick A. Praeger, Publishers, 1967).

15. Helmut Gollwitzer, "The Christian in the Search for World Order and Peace," in Matthews, ed., *Responsible Government in a Revolutionary Age,* p. 77.

16. *The New York Times,* Aug. 30, 1965.

17. *Newsweek,* Jan. 10, 1966.

18. *The New York Times,* April 27, 1966.

19. *Religion in Communist Dominated Areas,* V:38–40 (March 15, 1966).

20. *The New York Times,* April 29 and May 1, 1967.

CHAPTER XIII
DOES MAN HAVE A NATURE?

1. Giovanni Pico della Mirandola, *Oration on the Dignity of Man,* tr. by Charles Glenn Wallis (The Bobbs-Merrill Company, Inc., 1965), pp. 4–5.

2. Dewey, *Human Nature and Conduct,* p. 113.

3. *Ibid.*

4. *Ibid.,* p. viii.

5. John Dewey, *Freedom and Culture* (G. P. Putnam's Sons, 1939), p. 126.

6. Jean-Paul Sartre, "Existentialism Is a Humanism." This well-known lecture of 1946 is available in various translations. I am using the translation by Philip Mairet, reprinted in Walter Kaufmann, ed., *Existentialism from Dostoevsky to Sartre* (Meridian Books, The World Publishing Co., 1956). See p. 309.

7. *Ibid.,* p. 291.

8. *Ibid.,* p. 292.

9. *Ibid.*

10. *Ibid.,* p. 303.

11. Camus, *The Rebel,* p. 16.

12. *Ibid.,* p. 237.

13. *Ibid.,* p. 250.

14. Albert Camus, *The Plague* (Alfred A. Knopf, Inc., 1948); original French edition, *La Peste* (1947), p. 278.

15. *Ibid.*

16. Cf. pp. 99–100 above.

17. Tillich, *The Courage to Be,* p. 1.

18. *Ibid.,* p. 15.

19. *Ibid.,* p. 39.

20. Reinhold Niebuhr, *The Self and the Dramas of History* (Charles Scribner's Sons, 1955), p. 4.

21. *Ibid.*, p. 39.
22. *Ibid.*, p. 98.
23. Tillich, *The Courage to Be*, p. 82.
24. Reinhold Niebuhr, *The Self and the Dramas of History*, p. 65.
25. *Ibid.*, p. 67.
26. Mehl, *Images of Man*, pp. 51–52.

Chapter XIV
Is Man a Religious Being?

1. Arnold Toynbee, *An Historian's Approach to Religion* (Oxford University Press, Inc., 1956), p. 205.
2. Bonhoeffer, *Prisoner for God*, p. 122 (April 30, 1944).
3. *Ibid.*, p. 148 (June 8, 1944).
4. *Ibid.*, p. 123 (April 30, 1944). Barth in *The Epistle to the Romans* said that when God is assigned to the department of religion in human affairs, then "God has ceased to be God." (P. 79.)
5. Bonhoeffer, *Prisoner for God*, p. 123 (June 8, 1944).
6. Tillich describes this essay briefly in *The Protestant Era* (The University of Chicago Press, 1948), p. xvi. The untranslated essay was published in *Kantstudien*, XXVII (1922), pp. 446–469.
7. Tillich, *The Protestant Era*, p. 185.
8. Paul Tillich, *On the Boundary* (Charles Scribner's Sons, 1966), pp. 71, 73. The comments were originally published in 1936.
9. Paul Tillich, *Christianity and the Encounter of the World Religions* (Columbia University Press, 1963), p. 4.
10. Tillich, *The Protestant Era*, pp. xv–xvi. Tillich specifically vindicates the use of the phrase, "Biblical religion," against its critics in *Biblical Religion and the Search for Ultimate Reality* (The University of Chicago Press), pp. 1–5.
11. Bonhoeffer, *Prisoner for God*, pp. 147–148 (June 8, 1944).
12. *Ibid.*, pp. 132, 125 (May 21 and May 5, 1944).
13. *Ibid.*, p. 124 (April 30, 1944).
14. *Ibid.*, p. 146 (June 8, 1944).
15. *Ibid.*, p. 124 (April 30, 1944).
16. *Ibid.*, pp. 167–168 (July 18, 1944).
17. *Ibid.*, p. 177 (Aug. 3, 1944).
18. *Ibid.*, p. 185 (Aug. 23, 1944).
19. John A. T. Robinson, *Honest to God* (The Westmin-

ster Press, 1963), *passim*. An interesting evidence of Robinson's thinking is his index, in which there are many references to the following, listed here in the order of greatest number of references: Bonhoeffer, Tillich, and "Religionless Christianity."

20. Hoekendijk, *The Church Inside Out*, p. 59.
21. *Ibid.*, pp. 180–181.
22. Cox, *The Secular City*, pp. 2–3. In the revised edition of *The Secular City* (The Macmillan Company, 1966), Cox has modified his earlier comments on religion. I discovered this revision after sending this book to press. Rather than rewrite the proofs, I am letting my statements stand, since Cox's initial formulations set the terms of so many recent debates. But in fairness to a fertile and influential thinker, I call attention to his qualifications of his own definition of the issue.
23. *Ibid.*, pp. 62–63.
24. *Ibid.*, p. 262.
25. Goodman, "Student Chaplains," *The New Republic*, Vol. 156, No. 1 (Jan. 7, 1967), pp. 29–31.
26. Nathan A. Scott, Jr., *Ernest Hemingway: A Critical Essay* (Wm. B. Eerdmans Publishing Company, 1966), p. 42.

CHAPTER XV
HOW CONFIDENT HAS MAN A RIGHT TO BE?

1. "Foreword," in Bennett, ed., *Christian Social Ethics in a Changing World*, p. 18.
2. *Ibid.*, pp. 18–19.
3. Paul Abrecht, "The Development of Ecumenical Social Ethics," *ibid.*, p. 163.
4. Cox, *The Secular City*, pp. 58, 125.
5. *Ibid.*, p. 128.
6. William Hamilton, "Thursday's Child," in Thomas J. J. Altizer and William Hamilton, *Radical Theology and the Death of God* (The Bobbs-Merrill Company, Inc., 1966), p. 87.
7. Hamilton, "The New Optimism—from Prufrock to Ringo," in Altizer and Hamilton, *Radical Theology and the Death of God*, p. 156.
8. *Ibid.*, p. 168.
9. Joseph Wood Krutch, *The Modern Temper* (Harcourt, Brace & Co., Inc., 1929), pp. 88–89.
10. Joseph Wood Krutch, *The Measure of Man* (The Bobbs-Merrill Company, Inc., 1954).

198 NEW DIRECTIONS IN THEOLOGY TODAY, VOL. VI

11. James Reston, "Washington: The New Pessimism," *The New York Times*, April 21, 1967.

12. Thomas J. J. Altizer, "Theology and the Contemporary Sensibility," in William A. Beardslee, ed., *America and the Future of Theology* (The Westminster Press, 1967), p. 15.

13. Thomas J. J. Altizer, *The Gospel of Christian Atheism* (The Westminster Press, 1966), p. 144; cf. p. 128.

14. Chad Walsh, *From Utopia to Nightmare* (Harper & Row, Publishers, Inc., 1963).

15. Hamilton, "The New Optimism—from Prufrock to Ringo," in Altizer and Hamilton, *Radical Theology and the Death of God*, p. 169.

16. Malcolm Muggeridge, address at investiture as Rector of Edinburgh University, Scotland. *The New York Times*, Feb. 19, 1967.

17. See pp. 27–28 above.

18. Paul Goodman, *Utopian Essays and Practical Proposals* (Vintage Books, Random House, Inc., 1964).

19. Hamilton, "The New Optimism—from Prufrock to Ringo," in Altizer and Hamilton, *Radical Theology and the Death of God*, p. 159.

20. Carl Becker, *The Heavenly City of the Eighteenth-Century Philosophers* (Yale University Press, 1932), p. 31.

21. Brinton, *Ideas and Men*, p. 369.

22. William Hamilton, "The Death of God," *Playboy*, Aug. 1966, p. 138.

23. Cox, *The Secular City*, pp. 129–130.

24. Saul Bellow, *The Adventures of Augie March* (Crest Books, Fawcett Publications, Inc., 1965), p. 299.

25. See Charles C. West, "What It Means to Be Secular," *Christianity and Crisis*, XXV:147–149 (1965); and "Cox on His Critics," pp. 274–275.

26. J. M. Lochman, "The Service of the Church in a Socialist Society," in Bennett, ed., *Christian Social Ethics in a Changing World*, pp. 232–233.

27. Hoekendijk, *The Church Inside Out*, p. 60.

28. *Ibid.*, pp. 81, 188–189.

CHAPTER XVI
WHAT ABOUT SIN?

1. Richard L. Rubenstein, "Thomas Altizer's Apocalypse," in Beardslee, ed., *America and the Future of Theology*, pp. 37–40. Cf. Rubenstein, *After Auschwitz: Radical Theology*

and Contemporary Judaism (The Bobbs–Merrill Company, Inc., 1966).

2. Walter Rauschenbusch, *Christianizing the Social Order* (The Macmillan Company, 1912), p. 30.

3. Reinhold Niebuhr, *The Nature and Destiny of Man,* Vol. I, Ch. 7.

4. Reinhold Niebuhr, *Beyond Tragedy* (Charles Scribner's Sons, 1941), pp. 156–157.

5. J. William Fulbright, *The Arrogance of Power* (Vintage Books, Random House, Inc., 1966), pp. 3–4.

6. Edmund Stillman and William Pfaff, *Power and Impotence* (Random House, Inc., 1966).

7. Walter Lippmann, "Today and Tomorrow," *New York World Journal Tribune,* March 16, 1967.

8. Hamilton, "The New Optimism—from Prufrock to Ringo," in Altizer and Hamilton, *Radical Theology and the Death of God,* p. 169.

9. *Ibid.,* p. 165. Cox, unlike Hamilton, relates his hopefulness to passages in Paul. See *The Secular City,* pp. 129–130.

CHAPTER XVII
WHO IS MAN, AND WHAT IS HUMANISM?

1. Aristotle, *Politics,* I, 3.

2. Bonhoeffer, *Prisoner for God,* p. 183 (Aug. 21, 1944).

3. Abraham J. Heschel, *The Insecurity of Freedom* (The Jewish Publication Society of America, 1966), p. 23.

4. Keniston, *The Uncommitted,* p. 429.

5. Julian Huxley, "The Future of Man—Evolutionary Aspects," in Wolstenholme, ed., *Man and His Future,* pp. 1, 22.

6. Loren Eiseley, "Man: The Lethal Factor," address before the American Association for the Advancement of Science, Dec., 1962. Printed in *The Key Reporter,* Spring, 1963.

7. Alfred North Whitehead, *The Function of Reason* (Princeton University Press, 1929), p. 7.

8. Fyodor Dostoevsky, *The Brothers Karamazov,* tr. by Constance Garnett (Modern Library, Inc., 1943), p. 283 (Book V, Ch. 4).

9. Konrad Lorenz, *On Aggression* (Harcourt, Brace & World, Inc., 1966).

10. Ashley Montagu, "Original Sin Revisited: A Reply to Recent Popular Theories on Aggression," *Vista* (United Nations Association of the U.S.A.), Vol. II, No. 4 (Jan.–Feb., 1967), p. 47.

11. John Dewey, *A Common Faith* (Yale University Press, 1934), pp. 53–54.

12. Bentley Glass, *Science and Ethical Values* (University of North Carolina Press, 1965), p. 76.

13. Roberts, *The Scientific Conscience*, p. 104.

14. Artur Glikson, "Man's Relationship to His Environment," in Wolstenholme, ed., *Man and His Future*, p. 143.

15. Boulding and Clark, *Human Values on the Spaceship Earth*, p. 6.

16. *Ibid.*, p. 14.

17. Toynbee, *An Historian's Approach to Religion*. The description of the three types of man-worship is in Chs. 3, 4, and 5. The quotations are from Ch. 6, pp. 77, 78.

18. H. Richard Niebuhr, *Radical Monotheism and Western Culture*, p. 37.

19. Rudolf Bultmann, "Humanism and Christianity," *The Journal of Religion*, XXXII:77 (1952).

20. *Ibid.*, p. 83. It would be an instructive but complex task to compare this lecture of Bultmann's with Heidegger's short book, *Über den Humanismus* (Frankfurt: Klostermann, 1947). Bultmann's dependence upon and independence of Heidegger are both evident in the comparison.

21. Bultmann, "Humanism and Christianity," *The Journal of Religion*, XXXII:83 (1952).

22. *Ibid.*, p. 86.

23. Erich Fromm, "Introduction," in Fromm, ed., *Socialist Humanism: An International Symposium* (Doubleday & Company, Inc., 1965), p. vii. The capital "H" in Humanists is in the original.

24. H. Richard Niebuhr, *The Responsible Self* (Harper & Row, Publishers, Inc., 1963), p. 56.

25. Helmut Thielicke, *Theologische Ethik* (Tübingen: J. C. B. Mohr, 1951–1964), Vol. I, par. 705, *et passim*.

26. Lehmann, *Ethics in a Christian Context*, p. 58.

27. Erich Fromm, *Man for Himself* (Rinehart & Co., Inc., 1947).

28. Lochman, "The Service of the Church in a Socialist Society," in Bennett, ed., *Christian Social Ethics in a Changing World*, pp. 238–239.

29. Spike, *To Be a Man*, p. 123.

Index